About the Author

Michael Loyd Gray is the author of the novel *The Canary*, a Pushcart Prize nominee (2013) revealing Amelia Earhart's final days. His novel *Exile on Kalamazoo Street* was released in 2015 by Coffeetown Press. He is also the author of the novel *Not Famous Anymore,* 2011, which was awarded a grant by the Elizabeth George Foundation, and the novels, *Well Deserved* (2008 Sol Books Prose Series Prize) and *King Biscuit* (Tempest, 2012). Gray won the 2005 *Alligator Juniper Fiction Prize* and the 2005 *The Writers Place Award for Fiction.* He earned a MFA from Western Michigan University, a bachelor's degree from the University of Illinois, and has taught at colleges and universities in Illinois, Texas, and New York. For nearly ten years he was a staff writer for newspapers in Arizona and Illinois. Big orange cats, the Chicago Bears, and the Rolling Stones are among the constants in his life.

Michael Loyd Gray

SORT OF STILL ORIGINAL IN UNORIGINAL TIMES

AUSTIN MACAULEY
PUBLISHERS LTD.

A CIP catalogue record for this title is available from the British Library.

ISBN 9781786295538 (Paperback)
ISBN 9781786295545 (Hardback)
ISBN 9781786295552 (E-Book)
www.austinmacauley.com

First Published (2016)
Austin Macauley Publishers Ltd.
25 Canada Square
Canary Wharf
London
E14 5LQ

Acknowledgments

I have no agent to thank for the publication of this book. But I *had* an agent – two of them, in fact: Pauline Vilain died unexpectedly a couple of years ago before she could see this book in print. She encouraged me to write it and was a good friend. Siobhan McBride represented me briefly, after Pauline, before moving on from being an agent, which saddened me because I loved working with her in that brief time. Both ladies helped me as a writer.

I want to once more thank my mother, Dorothy Gray, for having faith in me when others had none.

Writers usually have a mentor, or mentors, and I had several: Stuart Dybek, Daniel Curley, and Monique Raphel High. I appreciate the great advice I got from all three of them.

Thanks to my two devilish cats, Suzie Lucifer and Yoda Lucifer, for keeping me company. The Lucifer Sisters are the generation following two very dear, departed cats – E.H. and Moonpie.

EARLY DAYS AND THE FAME GAME

The Time I Met Alice Cooper
(I Think)

Memory's a funny thing. What we remember isn't always accurate. Hell, sometimes what we remember isn't even true, even though we want it to be. Does that still make it a memory? A delusion? Republican ideology? I'm not sure. What was it Mark Twain once said – something about having lived through terrible times and some of them actually happened? I know the feeling, though this isn't about a terrible time at all.

Memory tells me that I met Alice Cooper. You know, Vincent Damon Furnier from Detroit – the scariest guy in rock and roll. No More Mr. Nice Guy, runny mascara, the boa constrictor lounging menacingly around his neck. That's the claim, anyway. Nowadays he's more like a conservative capitalist and plays golf a lot. But back then, he was Alice Fucking Cooper. The Dark Prince of Rock and Roll.

I met Alice at the long bar in J. Muncy's, a clean, well-lit (if I may borrow from Hemingway) yuppie eatery on Camelback Road in Phoenix. I never thought of myself as a yuppie, but I certainly liked the yuppie women who went there. J. Muncy's isn't even there anymore, but in the mid-80s it thrived and I was a regular and probably knew every bartender and server. It was around the time of that great '85 Bears team. I was then a staff writer for the *Arizona Business Gazette,* which was the weekly business paper owned by *The Arizona Republic.* And Alice was Alice. Very famous. A Phoenix icon. I don't recall if this was before he stopped drinking. I was definitely drinking – whiskey. In those days, Canadian Club on the rocks.

Rocket fuel.

In those days, I was also living a little like Keith Richards, but not necessarily gifted with his ability to transcend substance abuse. And if Alice was still drinking, then he was yet to learn that big lesson, too. That particular evening at J. Muncy's, my sense of it was that Alice came in with his wife and she sat in a booth and he came up to the bar. Maybe to stretch his legs, get the lay of the land.

Meeting Alice Cooper is different than, say, meeting Gene Simmons without Kiss makeup. I've never met Simmons, but I feel sure this is true: without makeup, Simmons looks like just another greedy, old, rich guy with a bad haircut trying to be twenty-five again. But Alice without make up pretty much looks the same as his stage counterpart. Like Keith Richards, Alice doesn't really need much makeup. When Keef did his *Pirates of the Caribbean* cameo as Capt. Jack Sparrow's father, I wondered whether he even required a wardrobe change or make up at all. Keith was asked to play himself – a pirate.

But back to Alice, as much fun as Keith Richards is. I think that when Alice came up to the bar from his booth he stood one or two stools away. I don't think anyone else was at the bar. It was late afternoon, but before the happy hour crowd had begun to drift in. I looked at him, and he looked at me and nodded pleasantly. I turned back for a sip of my drink and it hit me: Alice Fucking Cooper. School's Out, baby. I looked back at him and he knew that look. He knew I knew who he was. It had likely happened a million times to him. This was well before Wayne and Garth telling him they weren't worthy.

I blurted out something clever: "You're Alice Cooper."

He just smiled wearily, which was a good answer.

It would have been great timing had "School's Out" come on the jukebox at that moment.

It's still a very cool song.

But it didn't.

I should have rushed over and played it.

But I didn't.

And I have no idea whether it was even on the jukebox.

So, I asked Alice how he felt about the weather, which I don't now recall. In Phoenix the weather is either Hell, just short of Hell, or pleasant for a couple of minutes. You make gallows conversation about the first two and talk with relief about the other. Surprisingly, Alice was friendly and we did talk about the weather, whichever one it was, and then about J. Muncy's, which was a popular but not pretentious watering hole. James Garner and Sally Field once dropped in for dinner after filming *Murphy's Romance* down by Florence. Willie Nelson dropped in one night, too. And of course it was *my* hangout and so you know it was a cool place.

My chat with Alice lasted several minutes and he didn't seem in a rush to brush me off. He smiled and talked casually like someone who enjoyed the small talk. Then he went back to his wife in the booth.

But that's not the end of the story.

Not long after that, either a few weeks or a few months, I was invited to a pretty upper-class party because of people I knew in public relations through my job as a reporter. I went, of course, because I hoped to meet women better than the ones I met at J. Muncy's, which weren't bad, but one can always hope to climb higher, I suppose. At the party I went to the bar for a drink – Canadian Club on the rocks, of course – and when I turned around with my drink, there leaning against a wall was Alice Fucking Cooper.

I almost didn't go over, but I did because I knew standing next to Alice Fucking Cooper would make me cool by association if not in reality. And because this was an invitation-only soiree, Alice likely wasn't too worried about star struck fans trying to soap him up, and so as I approached he smiled – for a scary guy he really had a nice smile – and I asked him about the weather since I was obviously a gifted conversationalist.

He stared at me a moment and then said, "Don't I know you?"

I was still digesting the notion that Alice Cooper was claiming to know me and he said, "Yeah – J. Muncy's. I know you from Muncy's."

Suddenly, Alice Fucking Cooper and I were buddies. Soon we'd be jamming, I figured, though I hadn't played bass guitar since junior high school.

"Muncy's – yes," was all I could initially manage.

I think he surely must have felt that if I was at this exclusive party then I must, at the very least, not be retarded and even okay to talk to. I was *worthy*, to borrow again from Wayne and Garth. And we had J. Muncy's as a point of reference, our connection – where we *hung out*. I don't recall much of what we talked about. I wish I did. I do think we chatted nicely for a bit and I probably asked him what he liked best about Phoenix because at some point I remembered I was a newspaper reporter and could maybe turn it all into a story – like the time I did the last interview with the late novelist Erskine Caldwell in Scottsdale, which is a later chapter.

All I still have is this fragment in my head, like a still photograph, of chatting with Alice Cooper like we had known each other for years. It's always been a pretty bright fragment in my head.

And over the years I have told this story dozens of times – mostly to impress women, and sometimes it does.

But because I have always had an active imagination, and because I'm a novelist and love to make things up, I'm not entirely sure now if any of it happened at all.

Go ask Alice.

But I'm keeping my memory.

The Time I Almost Met Stevie Nicks (But Didn't)

This memory I'm pretty sure about. Honest. I can't say why I'm so sure, but I am. I have my moments of lucidity. One night when I was watching TV in my Phoenix apartment, a friend of mine called from a bar. I can't recall the bar's name or what was on TV.

My friend says, "Get down here right now – Stevie Nicks is sitting at the bar."

I paused, had a thought, and said, "Is Alice Cooper with her?"

He paused and said, "Alice Cooper? No. I don't see Alice Cooper anywhere."

"Are you sure?" I said.

"Yeah, I'm sure," he said. "I think I'd know if Alice Fucking Cooper was sitting here."

"Look around the room," I said. "Are you really sure?"

Another pause. I figured he was drunk.

"Jesus – yes, I'm sure. I'm looking now – there ain't no Alice Cooper."

"Are you sure it's really Stevie Nicks?"

Now, I was actually thinking that it *might* be her because I had read in some Phoenix magazine that Stevie Nicks was known to frequent that bar and I also felt that my friend was not particularly insane or retarded.

"It's her," he said. "It's Stevie Fucking Nicks. Okay? I'm looking at her, man. The hair, the long dress, the whole Stevie Nicks fucking shebang."

"What do you want me to do about it?" I said.

"Get down here," he said. "Ain't you a reporter?"

My friend was a sales rep for an alcohol distributor and he was drunk a lot and so while I could believe he thought he saw her, and I suspected that that would be the place if she really was there, I was a little skeptical.

"Really – it's her?" I said.

"What am I – delusional?" he said.

"Probably drunk."

"Just come down here now," he said. "It's only a few minutes."

That was true: it was a very short drive and I made it in record time. I found Steve at the bar and I looked around, but I didn't see Stevie Nicks.

"She was sitting right there," he said, pointing to a place a few stools away.

Celebrities always seem to be sitting just a few stools away, I thought absently.

I looked back toward the door.

"Is she in the bathroom?"

"No. She took off."

"When?"

"A few minutes ago – you just missed her."

Celebrities always seem to have left just a few minutes ago, I thought absently.

I sat down and ordered rocket fuel – Canadian Club on the rocks.

"Was she really here?" I said after my first sip. "Or did you just want someone to drink with?"

He shook his head.

"It was her. Don't you think I know Stevie Nicks when I see her?"

"Sure. Sure you do."

I drank some more of my drink and decided a couple more wouldn't be bad at all and now I had a friend to drink with. I looked around the room one more time and said, "Are you sure you didn't see Alice Cooper?"

They Told Me I Was There

"I was born in a crossfire-hurricane
And I howled at my ma in the driving rain"
−The Rolling Stones

Well, obviously it wasn't *that* bad. Not even close. There were no hurricanes, no tornadoes − no Mick Jagger. But how would *I* know? Who the hell remembers being born? I don't. All I can say is, they told me I was there. A featured role. They couldn't start without me. The room waited patiently for my entrance. The orchestra fidgeted and waited for the diva. There were witnesses and papers got signed and everything probably smelled like antiseptic. The doctor maybe forgot about golf for a minute. And perhaps a nurse had second thoughts on motherhood. I should ask my mother what the weather was like that day. There's a sleepy-looking, tiny alien in old photographs that people swear is me as a baby. I disagree, but I concede that it's *someone*.

They say it all began at St. Francis Catholic Hospital in Jonesboro, Arkansas. May 29, 1952 − the same birthday as President John F. Kennedy and right there I guess the similarities end, though it's a fact I never go to Dallas in November, and I've never owned a convertible. And unlike JFK, we weren't Catholic. My mom is Baptist, though that never took with me. More on this in a later chapter to be called God or Religion or Snake Oil. About twelve years later I was in that same hospital again with a broken arm, which ruined me as a shortstop, but I don't recall anyone at the hospital reminding me I was born there. Still, I'm taking everyone's word on it. Would they all lie about this?

Now, I'm a Southerner by birth, but not by upbringing. When I was about a year old my mother got a divorce, married someone else, and we moved to a place on the South Side of Chicago that my friend, writer Stuart Dybek, would many years later tell me was a bad area indeed. You know, a place Al Capone might have felt comfortable in and maybe he did. I should look into that. But that was before my time. And so, like my birth – no memories whatsoever of Chicago. I don't think there are even any photographs. I don't recall seeing any. It was a place where my mother was told to keep the door locked and don't open it for anybody. At least she didn't have to worry about Al Capone. I should check to see how good the Bears were that year.

After that year behind locked doors in Chicago, we moved to downstate Champaign, which in those days was a university surrounded quietly by corn, cows, and conservatives. It still is, though it's grown quite a bit and now you can at least get a decent beer there. And the conservatives have had to let some reality and the modern world intrude into their bubbles. Right now as I write, I am starting to remember things: my stepfather had a huge train set in the basement of our house, which I can actually now picture in my head. It was a white two-story on Harris Street next to railroad tracks. A junior high school was just a couple blocks away. I think there was a vacant lot across the street. With some neighborhood kids, I helped build a snow fort one winter next to the railroad tracks and the fort had narrow ice caves and there were the kind of snowball fights that left faces pink and frozen.

Come to think of it, my grandparents' house in Arkansas was next to railroad tracks. Even now, here in Kalamazoo, Michigan, as I write this, I can hear the AMTRAK train to Chicago from my house at night. When I was a graduate student at Western Michigan University here in Kazoo, that Chicago train ran practically through my kitchen. And come to think of it, my grandfather was a lineman on the Cotton Belt Railroad.

So, what's this train conspiracy all about and who is behind it?

But back to the Harris Street days. We didn't live there long and I don't recall any other details about it. Soon we moved to the house we would live in as a family for a long time, the house on Campbell Street. In those days our neighborhood was several miles outside Champaign and our backyard bordered an abandoned dairy farm. Pheasants were known to fly out of thick underbrush just across the backyard fence. A huge hedge apple tree towered over our backyard and the foul-smelling green "apples" as large as softballs littered our yard. I used to see how far I could toss them out into the cornfields and I often pretended I was an outfielder tossing the long ball all the way to home plate to catch the runner from third.

I committed my first – and really only – serious larceny (bubble gum at the IGA grocery store doesn't really count) soon after we moved to Campbell Drive: when the dairy farm behind our house was torn down, a large and noisy Pepsi-Cola plant was built there. One day Steve _____ and I scaled a wire fence as though we were saboteurs in a James Bond film and we snuck between two Pepsi delivery trucks and stole a case of Pepsi. How we managed to get back over that fence without getting caught or even noticed was a miracle.

Our act was certainly juvenile delinquency, but well short of Jesse James or John Dillinger territory. We were about twelve years old, I think. Perhaps thirteen. I never knew what happened to Steve. His family moved away soon after that. Maybe our caper sparked a serious career in crime and he's in prison somewhere wishing he had a cold Pepsi. When I think of that day, I remind myself that if someone's going to steal a case of anything, at least make it a case of beer.

The Campbell Drive house had a basketball goal above the garage, but it fell short of regulation height. And the backboard was always too loose, which made it even harder to hit a bank shot. Neighborhood kids showed up often to shoot hoops and games often lasted until it got dark and ended only when everyone gave up on making a basket without really seeing the goal. The house had a little brick patio out back with a light pole – a cheap imitation of London street lamps from the 1800s, as I recall – and at night in good weather it was a pleasant place to sit and listen to the cricket symphony. Beyond the backyard fence, farm fields stretched to the horizon. I played soldier in those fields with neighborhood boys.

Our phone number at that house was 352-6842. I can't believe I still remember that number when I can't recall the addresses or numbers of places when I lived in upstate New York or Texas or California. I do remember the Campbell Street house very well. It was a white bi-level with a long, slanting roof, and in the winter if a lot of snow piled up, us kids would slide down the roof into snowdrifts. In better weather my friends and I would climb up there to see if we could catch a glimpse of the girls next door changing clothes in their bedrooms – maybe I'll reveal the results in a later chapter. I think Steve climbed up there with me once and so you can see

I was definitely exposed to crime and perversion early on, but managed to avoid a career of it, though mild perversion can make for a serviceable hobby.

Once, on a gorgeous summer day, I went to the very top of the roof, and because that part of Illinois is flatter than your third-grade cousin and less interesting than your aunt who knits blankets, I had what passed for a view. Scenery. Landscape. A vista. If you like corn and soybeans, that is. From my perch I could see an old two-lane highway that disappeared out toward Mahomet and the Sangamon River. Out there was the closest thing to actual good country unless you drove much further south. From the roof I could look out over endless cornfields shimmying in the breeze and imagine Chicago far to the north and St. Louis far to the southwest. Indianapolis was to the east.

Up on the roof, I began to suspect just how big the world might be.

Erskine Caldwell
(*Tobacco Road* and *God's Little Acre* in Case You Forgot)

Another accurate story. Yes, I actually knew Erskine Caldwell, a writer whose work is largely, and sadly, forgotten these days. It was during my Arizona years – you know, living on the surface of the sun. When I told writer Daniel Curley that I met Caldwell in Arizona, he looked perplexed and said, "Really? I thought he was dead."

A chapter on Dan Curley is coming. I have fond memories of him. He won the Flannery O'Connor Award one year and that's nothing to sneer at unless the person who wins it is someone you don't like. Then sneering is okay. I think Groucho Marx would have agreed.

And as it turned out, Caldwell did die not long after I interviewed him for the *Arizona Business Gazette,* but I certainly had nothing to do with it. I think it may be true that I did the last interview with him, but he looked okay when I left. Honest.

Anyway, before I met Erskine, I knew his wife, Virginia. I had just moved to Arizona and I got a job in a Scottsdale bookstore in one of those impossibly pretentious Scottsdale malls where rich people believe they really are gods. One day I heard that Rod Stewart was spotted walking around, doing whatever Rod

Stewart would do at a mall, maybe asking random women whether they liked his body and thought he was sexy, to paraphrase the song, but I didn't see him and so I can't really stretch that into much of a chapter. But maybe I could manage a few paragraphs about how Rod Stewart was once a great rock singer who eventually became more like that lounge lizard singer Bill Murray portrayed on Saturday Night Live.

But back to the Caldwells. This hoity-toity Scottsdale mall was called The Borgata. But it ain't no strip mall, folks. There's no Big Lots or Dollar General there. I guess the rich lords wanted to pretend they were in Italy and certainly the weather would have been better in Italy. But if you're rich, why are you living in the middle of a desert? Thank God I only had to work in that bookstore a couple months before landing my first newspaper job. But I'm thankful I did work there for a short time because I met Virginia Caldwell. A very nice woman. When she told me who she was and about Erskine, my first thought was the same as Dan Curley's reaction – I figured Caldwell was long since dead.

Virginia frequented the store and we became friends, even after I moved on to my job with the *Arizona Business Gazette*. Once she even called me in the newspaper newsroom to tell me she had just been reading some Hemingway and wanted to talk about him.

"Uh, Virginia – I'm sort of in the middle of a story here," I said, though I must admit that nothing I was writing about for the paper was even as remotely interesting as Hemingway and Caldwell. Not ever. Writing about businesses and notable business folks quickly became limiting and boring, just as it was a few years later when I worked for a daily newspaper and wrote about sewer districts, lame and selfish local conservative politicians, and other coma-inducing events.

But back to dear Virginia, which makes me now think of a Rolling Stones song: *Sweet Virginia*. Anyway, rich people have a different sense of time and obligation, but naturally I put my story aside to chat with Virginia. She really was a delight and I genuinely liked her. And that really paid off because no one could get an interview with Erskine – except me. One day Virginia called and invited me to the house to meet him.

I used to have several photographs taken by a newspaper photographer of my meeting with Caldwell, but they disappeared. It was a sunny day and no doubt winter because in the photographs I'm wearing a long-sleeve shirt and I think he wore a sweater. If it had been summer, people would have walked around wishing they were naked. Anyway, we sat in comfortable chairs on his patio and drank lemonade. Caldwell looked very serious and quite attentive in the photographs. He was leaning forward from his chair, elbows on his knees, watching me closely. I think maybe he was just doing his best to endure an interview he didn't want to do and was being diplomatic to please his wife. He was a Southerner and had a sense of hospitality and etiquette that reminded me of my cousins in Arkansas.

I actually first met him in his study. Virginia took me there and introduced us and quickly left, and Caldwell slowly got out of the chair behind his desk and offered a hand. He was very tall and I recalled at that moment that he had once played semi-professional football.

After we shook hands he said, "Here to do an interview, are you?"

"Yes, sir."

He studied me a moment, a bit coldly, and said, "Well, good luck with that."

I was a bit intimidated, but he smiled finally and then suggested we sit outside.

At first, Erskine was slow to warm up to the interview. He appeared capable of only short answers and a stone face, and he looked away often, seeming distracted, as he pondered how to reply. I think the ice breaker was his famous short story, "Where the Girls Were Different." I had always liked that story and I told him so and what I liked about it, which I don't now recall, but it's a nice little story and he perked up and talked about it with some animation and even smiled. I sensed that he had not thought of that story or talked about it for many years and that he rather enjoyed doing so. I still think that he finally warmed up to me because he could see I knew his work and appreciated it and I was not just another reporter looking to step across his mother's grave to get a scoop.

But the scoop was nice, too.

I don't recall the rest of the conversation. But the interview was published and perhaps if there is an archive at the *Arizona Republic*, which then owned the now defunct *Arizona Business Gazette*, that interview still exists. I no longer have a copy. The interview was considered quite the scoop and the publisher of the *Arizona Republic* sent around a note of congratulations to our managing editor.

Not so long after that glorious scoop, the managing editor was nonetheless forced out in some senseless administrative coup, and by the next year, I believe it was, I quit the newspaper to take a job in California. Erskine had died and I never saw Virginia again.

Crossroads

This isn't about the immortal song by Robert Johnson or even versions by Eric Clapton, or Jimi Hendrix, or Duane Allman, or anybody else, though that would be fun to talk about. It's certainly not about Karl Rove and his fascist American Crossroads and its intolerant agenda for re-making America into something more like the former Soviet Union.

This is about a crossroads in life.

Perhaps my first.

I've already mentioned that I broke my arm as a kid. I was about twelve. Or thirteen. Or eleven. I'll ask my mom about that and adjust the age if need be later in the book.

It was a bad break.

It hurt like hell, or like the dickens, or like sin, or whatever you prefer.

I think I prefer, hurt like a sonofabitch.

The elbow shattered.

Ouch!

I tripped and fell from my grandmother's front porch in Jonesboro, Arkansas.

A damn high porch.

I landed smack on the elbow.

Ouch!

At the hospital I guess there was some talk about amputation.

Ouch!

Luckily, a doctor – Dr. Gray and no relation – managed to glue the pieces back together and now my elbow works fine.

No masturbation jokes, please.

And it got me out of serving in Vietnam.

That's a future chapter.

But I was in a cast for a year. That's an eternity to a kid, especially with a damn long pin inserted into the elbow joint to help keep the shattered pieces together to heal. The cast itched a lot. It could be agonizing. And my arm atrophied and I had to lift weights when it was all over to get it back in good shape. When I visited a friend on a farm outside Champaign, somehow I got corn kernels down in the cast and had a devil of a time getting them out. And the cast had my arm frozen in position as though I was Napoleon trying to stick a hand into a waistcoat. Baseball was over for good. And I used to be pretty good at tossing a ball. I was then in Farm League baseball and there would be no more of it. But I do still have my Tom Tresh (New York Yankees) mitt. It's battered and faded and seems much smaller than when I played with it. I love how it smells. It sits on the fireplace mantle with the ashes of two beloved cats – EH and Moonpie. More chapters to come.

I seem to recall spending much time in my room during that year in a cast. Time dragged on very slowly. Sometimes someone would stop by to see me. My room was in the front of the house facing the street and the bedroom window was low enough for someone standing to almost be able to look in. I often sat there by the window looking out at the shrubs below and the two trees in our front yard, and from there I could see all the way to the corner where Campbell Street met what was called Frontage Road. Beyond that was U.S Highway 150, which later became Interstate 74. In the other direction I could look down Campbell Street a good ways, too. In those days we only had three TV channels and so looking out the window didn't always fall that short of watching TV.

There wasn't much to do and so I read. I actually had the entire Hardy Boys series. It wasn't great literature, but it was reading and the more one reads, the better they get at it, and at some point it may have even occurred to me that it could be fun to write something, too.

But I won't claim that was when I decided to be a writer.

That came much later.

But I think that may have been when I first read *The Old Man and the Sea*, which had not been out all that many years and I am fairly sure it was one of the first really serious works of fiction I read. I was starting to see how a book could address some weighty issues. There was magic in the Hemingway cadence that even then I was picking up on a little. Today I value the proper cadence in my writing quite a bit. Writing is music. Words are notes.

That time in a cast was long and it sort of forced me to slow down a bit and think about where everything was headed. I began to read more and more ambitiously. And even though I was always a poor student all the way through high school, thanks to a lack of interest in rules, I nonetheless began to see that I excelled in English. I could pretty much always write in complete sentences and I knew how to spell. It wasn't hard for me at all the way it was for many other kids and the way math is indeed very hard for me.

Math has always been impossible for me.

Math always seemed like a secret language with rules changing every five seconds.

But English – I got it.

I went from the bottom of my high school class to eventually finishing graduate school with a 3.93 GPA and as a Phi Kappa Phi National Honor Society scholar.

My high school journalism teacher predicted I would never even make it to college.

In fact, I believe I was the only one from that class who became a journalist.

Ten novels later, I think – not bad for a snotty kid who once had a hard time getting corn kernels out of his arm cast.

Jack Hemingway
(Yes, Ernest's Son)

I met Jack Hemingway in Sun Valley, Idaho. Hemingway Country. It was maybe 1986. Another true story with a photograph to go along with it – and yet I lost that photograph somewhere along the way, too. So, the lesson here is, don't give me any photographs you actually want to last.

But back to Jack, Ernest Hemingway's oldest son, and the one who seemed to achieve the most happiness – the most *normalcy* – of the three sons. I had been sent to Sun Valley by the paper to write skiing stories and my host there was with the chamber of commerce. When she found out I was a Hemingway fan, she called Jack at his house outside Sun Valley – caught him in the shower, he said – and he agreed to come into town to meet me.

I had a huge hangover the morning he so generously met me for breakfast at the Sun Valley Lodge. The night before I had perpetuated my best Ernest Hemingway drinking imitation on a prowl through several bars. But when I saw Jack enter the dining room with a broad smile, his face so reminiscent of his father's, I forgot about my hangover for a time and a sort of magical period of brushing up against history set in. I was stunned he would so spontaneously agree to come meet a stranger. And he really did resemble Ernest Hemingway.

Jack was relaxed and smiled often. He shared with me the news that the Hemingway family had recently discovered new photographs of his father from 1917 when he journeyed by canoe with his pal Ray Ohlsen out to Starved Rock State Park on the Illinois River, which is well west of Chicago. Jack was clearly delighted to talk about a new Hemingway discovery. He was quite pleased to have discovered something new about a father in which little was *not* known about his exploits.

Jack was so friendly and accommodating that I felt I could ask him about his father's suicide. He told me he understood it, that when his father lost his ability to write and enjoy life fully, that his life really was over. But rather wistfully he also said, "We Hemingways are a strange family." He also assured me that his father was indeed a very good father with a fun sense of humor around his sons. On long trips by car, Jack said, his father would keep him in stitches with jokes.

At some point I was no longer doing an interview and instead just listening to details about a family I have always found fascinating, and in a way that made me feel like I was closer to understanding the Hemingway legend than from any biography I had read. He seemed very comfortable telling me about his mother, his brothers, and his godmother in Paris in the 1920s – Gertrude Stein – and the time he was in a German POW camp in World War II. For a while I simply forgot to be hung over.

I asked Jack to tell me what it really was like to be in the orbit of such an extraordinarily famous man and he told me that of all the famous people he had met, which included Franklin Roosevelt and Winston Churchill, no one else had the charisma of his father, who was always the center of any room he was in.

Jack Hemingway had a good amount of that charisma, too.

I can still visualize him, walking away from the Sun Valley Lodge that morning, turning briefly to flash that smile and wave goodbye to me. He didn't seem to have minded at all that he had sat down with a stranger to talk about his 'strange' family.

I recently finished writing a novel called *The Canary*. It's about the last days of Amelia Earhart, but it also has an interior story set in Chicago in 1914-15 in which I give history a nudge and Ernest Hemingway meets Amelia Earhart while they were both in high school – Ernest in Oak Park and Amelia in Hyde Park. In *The Canary,* young Ernest Hemingway is already known for his great smile – a magnificent grin, as Amelia Earhart terms it – and when I met Jack Hemingway I knew exactly where he got *his* great smile, too.

Grade School, JFK, the White House
(Trust Me, There's a Connection)

I endured my grade school days at a tiny, isolated country school surrounded by cornfields. Seems like I have often been surrounded by cornfields, imprisoned by cornfields. Now I avoid corn for dinner.

I don't recall just why my parents thought it was a good idea to send me into farmland exile by bus every morning. I do recall the bus rides – the smell of exhaust and the chugging motor – and even part of the route as we stopped at farmhouses, sometimes to pick up just one freezing kid standing by the road on our way to Hensley School, which loomed rather naked and unprotected at an intersection of a two-lane highway and a blacktopped county road. There were few trees and everywhere the fields were flat, and when the wind blew hard, you really felt it. It cut like a knife.

Once you walked through the school's front door you were well on your way to its back door. I can now visualize much of the exterior and grounds, but very little of the interior except for a fuzzy image of a classroom with windows looking out over a very long playground with a farmhouse beyond. The playground field was wide enough and long enough that a football team could have scrimmaged on it. We sometimes played baseball or just kicked balls around. I think I recall exteriors from there better than interiors because I always daydreamed about escaping the place.

The only kid from those days I can recall is Bud Lange. His first name was actually Harris, but he went by Bud and I suppose most guys would if they had that first name, which didn't quite seem right for the early 1960s. The bus would pick Bud up at his house just a mile or so deep into the country route. His house was either the first stop or one of the first stops. I actually don't remember much more than that about Bud until junior high school. We both ended up at Jefferson Junior High, which was in Champaign proper. Bud grew into a sort of lanky guy and I remember very well that he wore Beatle Boots and had taps nailed to the heels which made a loud noise on the marble floors of the junior high school and they irritated the principal, Paul Sparks, to the point that he banned them – taps, not Beatle Boots, though many parents expressed concern over those, too.

After high school, Bud was killed in a car crash. I remember getting the news and absently wondering whether he was wearing his Beatle Boots at the time.

But this isn't about Bud. It's more about being in grade school in that tiny, conservative school in the country when President Kennedy was gunned down in Dallas. I recall vividly a teacher bursting into our classroom in tears and nearly shouting that the president had been killed. At first, all us kids just looked at each other. It was very quiet for a minute. All the adults in the school were out of sorts. I can't recall whether school was let out early or not. The assassination started to sink in with me pretty quickly because just the year before, I believe it was, my family had visited the White House. I think JFK may have even been there the day we took the tour. My mom was a big JFK fan and even took 8mm footage of him the day he came through Champaign in a motorcade. I think my mom can be termed a Kennedy liberal, at least back then, and I'm sure my own brand of liberalism stems from those days.

The coverage of the assassination was on TV and I was watching at the moment Jack Ruby gunned down Lee Harvey Oswald in a parking garage. It still ranks as one of the most stunning things I have ever seen. Over the years I became interested in all the efforts to suggest that JFK was killed by a conspiracy. I even met David Lifton, a well-known conspiracy theorist, and got to talk about it with him. He hinted strongly that he worried that Lyndon Johnson was behind it all. But nothing ever came of that. My mom went with me and we drove to Bloomington, Illinois, to hear Lifton speak and after his talk, he gave me the name of someone who lived in Hoopeston, Illinois, who had been in the emergency room the night JFK's body arrived at Bethesda Naval Hospital. I was a reporter for the newspaper in Champaign, which is a very Republican and partisan paper, and I wrote a story about the guy from Hoopeston, but it never saw the light of day.

I don't think we'll ever really know the whole truth about JFK. And I no longer think much about it. Now when I see an image of his head exploding in Dallas, I feel sad for a moment, and then it passes. Now it's simply history. I think the good in JFK outweighed the bad, but I just don't think much about him anymore. Really, the whole Camelot thing was a fantasy, just like Woodstock Nation proved to be a fantasy at tragic Altamont. America is a pretty tough place politically and it seems to me we are always going to be in danger of letting conservatives kill our democracy if we aren't vigilant.

I wonder if Bud Lange would have agreed.

Ron Jeremy
(Nina Hartley, Too – Yes, There's Actual Porn in This Book)

I met porn icon Ron Jeremy, a man with a famous penis, in Las Vegas around 1986 or so. I had flown up there from Phoenix to cover the Consumer Electronics Show for my newspaper. Most of the stuff I wrote about in those days was pretty boring capitalism indeed, but a chance to go to Vegas on the paper's dime was instant excitement. When I got there, I discovered my press credentials allowed me into the adult movies area. You know, actual porn star ladies walking around quite comfortably in skimpy bras and panties and high heels and chatting with fans. As with any job, I suppose people quickly get used to the uniform.

It was an odd sight as I entered the porn hall and saw many men, but a few women, too, clustered around nearly naked porn ladies who were obviously comfortable in their own skins because that was certainly what they were nearly down to. Imagine a football team suddenly huddling around the coach, who just happens to be a gorgeous woman in heels and the best Frederick's of Hollywood has to offer. No one was distracted from the object of the huddle. The men salivated and the few women looked on in curious admiration, I suppose. Maybe it was more than that.

I turned away from one huddle and nearly ran over Nina Hartley, who is a porn icon with a great mane of blond hair and who likely has had more sex in a month, and with more people, than some folks could ever imagine for themselves in a lifetime. With her history in mind, I decided that the bra, panties, and heels were actually more cover than she often maintained. I worked hard at keeping my eyes on her face.

"Are you enjoying yourself?" she said.

"I just got here," I said, realizing that sounded a little detached. "But it's interesting."

That didn't sound any better.

"And where did you come from?" Nina asked.

"Phoenix." It really was hard to keep eye contact. "I'm a reporter."

"Not a fan?" she said, glancing over her shoulder at a TV set up on a counter nearby. I glanced over at the set and saw a football game was on.

"Of football?" I said.

"That, too," she said, glancing at the game again.

"I love football," I said. "How about you?"

"Sure – why not," she said.

She kept glancing at the game and it dawned on me, as men discovered her and a horny huddle grew quickly around her, that she was like anyone else working a job, but also with a day-to-day life that included rooting for a team.

I slipped away from Nina – with some regret, of course -- and drifted toward a crowd at a counter. Several porn starlets were signing autographs on their pictures. At the end of the counter, a jowly man with long black hair was reading a newspaper. You don't have to be a porn expert to recognize Ron Jeremy – nowadays he even appears on reality shows. Can dating a Kardashian be in his future? And so there he was, not as fat as he is today, but certainly working on it and making much progress.

A fleshy man in a fleshy business.

We all know something about porn. Odd facts that become the catalysts for jokes, for example. Most people have seen porn, even if they won't admit it. Men who struggle to recall their wedding anniversaries are capable of looking up and exclaiming – "That's Nina Hartley! And she's almost naked!"

My odd porn fact: I had heard that Ron Jeremy – where in the world did I hear this? – was a teacher before he became famous (infamous?) for swinging a big sausage on film. It always struck me as unusual for a porn actor to start out as a teacher. Maybe there's more I should know about teachers I've worked with.

So I introduced myself to Mr. Jeremy, who was friendly, relaxed, a little bored, perhaps. After all, nearly naked ladies prancing around was business as usual for the guy. Just another day at the office – at the orifice, as the joke goes. I absently wondered whether he could stand next to Nina, watch the Browns, and not once recall how many times he'd had sex with her.

"You're Ron Jeremy," I said cleverly.

He rolled his eyes – it was subtle.

"Just call me Ron."

"Sure, Ron. So, is it really true you were a teacher before you got into adult films?"

"Yeah, I was. Back east."

When porn actors say they "worked" with someone, most of us tend to snigger like Beavis and Butthead. But apparently Ron Jeremy once lived out of the head on his shoulders instead of the one attached to his infamous appendage.

"From teacher to porn icon – quite a change of scenery," I said, nodding toward the porn starlets just down the counter from us.

"You noticed," he said, grinning.

A porn starlet pranced by and reached across the counter and squeezed one of Ron's cheeks – one of the cheeks on his face, that is.

"Love you, too, babe," Ron said.

For a moment I wondered how many times he had likely 'worked' with the porn babe. Then I asked the obvious question:

"So, what made you decide to get into porn, Ron?"

His grin expanded. "I have a big dick."

At that moment a man and woman in their forties, I guessed, rushed over to the counter, and the woman, shapely and well-preserved in a tight blue dress – a blond, if I recall correctly – eagerly asked Ron for his autograph and she touched his wrist and left her hand on it.

Ron Jeremy glanced at me and winked and signed his autograph.

I smiled back and walked away, understanding it all perfectly. Over by the TV on a counter, Nina Hartley, clad only in bra, panties, and heels, stood with arms crossed across her chest and watched the Cleveland Browns.

Elvis and Graceland
(The King!)

I grew up on Elvis.

That's a good thing, even though Elvis was a bit of a loveable wacko. I mean, look at how he dressed. Think Michael Jackson without the pedophilia. And where Jackson was just plain weird and not actually from this planet, Elvis was cool and likeable. If you can't like Elvis, then there's something wrong with you. If you don't like The King, then maybe you're a conservative, which means you only like gold doubloons and other rich, white men. Come to think of it, Elvis was a bit of a conservative, too: check out his impulsive trip to see Nixon to secure a law enforcement badge.

But Elvis was a rare strain of conservatism. You know, not uncomfortable around black people and he obviously never got the GOP memo about the dress code and haircuts.

And the boy could sing.

When I was a boy visiting grandparents and cousins in Arkansas, the adults would drop us kids at a theater in Jonesboro for an Elvis double feature. I don't recall titles and there's no need to because all Elvis movies are the same: he grins a lot, sings a lot, and romances gals a lot. Not bad work if you can get it. But they were great fun. And in those days if you bought an RC Cola at the theatre, you would look under your bottle cap and if there was a star, I believe it was, then you won some prize. We drank a lot of RC Cola. Dr. Pepper, too.

We went to Graceland when I was a kid – maybe eleven or twelve or thirteen. I guess a lot seemed to happen to me in those years. I recall the music notes on the gate to Graceland's drive. Pretty cool. I'd never seen anything like that before. I believe someone told us Elvis was at his home in California. For some reason I was carrying my skateboard with me that day. It may be that I skated Elvis's driveway. That sounds like something I would have done. A biographer once wrote that Elvis appeared to have furnished Graceland from roadside stands. The tour had limited access to the house and I can't really recall what it looked like inside.

My mom had a friend who once lived close to Graceland. I believe her yard ran close to Elvis's. According to the family legend, my mom's friend put her dog over the fence onto the Graceland property and later a grinning Elvis brought it back to her. I guess she used to see Elvis here and there around Memphis, and once, when he was driving a Jeep, he pulled alongside her at a light and waved and grinned and she sat stunned through the green light.

That's how it was back then when it came to Elvis, who was a sort of Boy God, especially in the South. Whenever he came on the movie screen, girls squealed and boys wished they could be just like him. Elvis appears in one of my novels. Any time you can work Elvis into a book or a conversation, it's a good thing.

It's an American thing.

I miss Elvis.

And John Lennon.

And George Harrison.

And Jimi Hendrix.

And Brian Jones.

And Janis Joplin.

And Duane Allman.

And Keith Moon.

And John Entwistle.

If there's a heaven, they've got one hell of a rock band up there.

George McGovern
(Yep, I Met That Dude, Too)

George McGovern died just a couple months before I wrote this. I met him around 1989 or 1990 or so when he gave a speech at the University of Illinois. I was a reporter for the local paper – a dreadful job for a dreadful paper. It was arranged for me to meet McGovern for a one-on-one interview either before or after the speech. I don't recall which it was. There was an awful lot about working for that paper that isn't worth remembering.

I arrived at a room in the university union building and while I waited, I scrutinized the many portraits on the wall. They were mostly fat cat types who had some connection to the university. Some were university officials and others I imagine just bought their way in. I have always liked looking closely at portraits and old photographs to see if I can get a palpable sense of the humanity of the people in them. I especially like to examine Civil War photographs because the people are so stiff and posed and it's hard to visualize them as also having been breathing and human and laughing and crying. I've been known to use a magnifying glass to try and bore in as close as I can to detect something human, something that indicates the person from history also was like me in some respects.

I became aware of someone else examining the portraits at the outer radar edge of my peripheral vision, and I believe I heard this person say that they recognized an acquaintance in one of the portraits. It sounded like a pleasant, unexpected discovery. I turned and there was George McGovern, the famous liberal candidate for president, a man some called a pacifist; but he was a pacifist in the best possible way because I knew he had flown many combat missions in World War II and was even shot down once. He knew about war in ways those chicken hawk conservatives who dodged serving – George W. Bush, Karl Rove, Dick Cheney, Dan Quayle – could never know because their approach to war is to sit it out and order the deaths of someone else's sons and daughters.

I knew that George McGovern, who could not get elected president, but George W. Bush, who was somehow elected twice – was a far better man than Bush and the rest of that conservative Praetorian Guard, and there he was, McGovern, smiling and pointing to a friend in a portrait, and then offering his hand to me.

Sadly, I don't have a copy of the story and I don't recall specifics. The newspaper may have the story archived, though, because McGovern was a liberal, I'm sure they'd charge for a copy. I do recall that McGovern was generous with his time and soft-spoken, thoughtful. We surely talked about his flying days in World War II because that stuff always fascinates me. No doubt we touched on his failed bid for the presidency. He might have made a fine president.

But it's hard for a good person to get elected in America – just ask Barack Obama.

Mickey Mantle and Roger Maris (Sort of Like Butch and Sundance with Bats)

Here's another tale from the early 1960s. As is often the case, I'm not sure of the exact date and year. Perhaps 1961. July, possibly. Doesn't matter. I looked up some baseball records for 1961 to see when the New York Yankees played the Chicago White Sox and there were plenty of games. I was at one of them, in old Comiskey Park on Chicago's South Side, sitting behind the Yankees' dugout. Perhaps only a few rows up. Really excellent seats. Much better than when I saw Hank Aaron play many years later.

My family and I drove up to Chicago from Champaign. That might have been my first time in Chicago when I was actually old enough to remember it. I would have been about nine or so. It was warm weather and we had the windows down. As we drove to Comiskey, a boy on a street corner had a straw and shot a pea or something like that into the car and hit my sister in the head. She wasn't hurt – just surprised. It was like an announcement – welcome to Chicago!

I have always thought that Whitey Ford pitched that day for the Yankees, but it also could have been Ralph Terry, for example, according to the records I saw. For the Sox, some legendary players took the field: Nellie Fox, Luis Aparicio, Minnie Minoso. And from where I sat behind the Yankees dugout, I had a brilliantly close view of Mickey Mantle and Roger Maris as they swung bats in the on-deck area. They were American heroes. Was it the Maris year of sixty-one homers? That would take research to determine. If it was indeed 1961, then, yes, it was. He broke Babe Ruth's record and his would stand for thirty-seven years. I can't recall how he and Mantle batted that day. No homers, I think, as I likely would remember such history. Yogi Berra was on that Yankees team. Tony Kubek, too. No doubt I'm omitting a few other notable players.

It doesn't matter that I don't recall how Mantle and Maris batted, or who won the game. I can look all that up. What matters is that I was there and witnessed priceless baseball history. It's almost as good as if I had witnessed the play of Shoeless Joe Jackson and Ty Cobb and Babe Ruth and Lou Gehrig and Joltin' Joe DiMaggio.

But not quite.

Falls a tad short.

Shoeless Joe and those others are the real golden age of baseball. Unforgettable characters and players.

Baseball now is boring to me. I don't follow it.

There's no Shoeless Joe or Mickey Mantle.

Maybe if they allowed tackling…

Not long after seeing Mantle and Maris I became a football fan for life.

Da Bears!

John Mackey
(Sad Story)

This is a story with a sad ending – two of them, actually. When I was a reporter in Arizona, someone arranged for me to do a phone interview with John Mackey, the former Baltimore Colts tight end. Some folks believe he was the greatest tight end in NFL history and I agree.

I think Mackey had just been in Phoenix for some business function and my paper covered business, and since he was famous, it was a good interview to get. It came out of the blue. I don't remember – are you sensing a pattern here? – who arranged it. A PR firm contact, I suspect. I seem to recall it was a tight window and a one-time deal – basically, be by a phone real damn soon and John Mackey will call you.

And he did. I attached a microphone to the phone and conducted the interview. It was exciting because I was a football fan and we talked about his playing days. He was friendly and talkative. I was using the microphone to record the interview because I knew I would have so much fun talking with a football legend that my note taking would suffer. I relished talking with someone who played for the real Colts – the Colts of Baltimore, if I may borrow some Hemingway phrasing, and not that team in Indianapolis that claims to be the Colts. Mackey played with Johnny Unitas, Tom Matte, Bubba Smith, Mike Curtis, and other legendary players.

After the interview I leaned back in my chair and basked in the glow of experiencing NFL greatness. I reached for the recorder and punched the button to play back the interview.

It did not record.

No interview.

If I ended up writing a story it was only something brief based on what I could recall.

I'm not convinced I wrote anything at all.

No timeless connection to John Mackey.

And sadly, John Mackey became afflicted with dementia before he died in 2011 at age sixty-nine.

Barry Goldwater
(Who May Have Believed in UFOs)

Yes, my path once crossed Barry Goldwater's. Another incident from my Arizona days as a reporter. One day my phone rang at my desk and when I answered, the very serious voice at the other end asked who I was and announced very firmly that he was Barry Goldwater.

I knew it had to be a prank.

"Oh, sure," I said. "How's it going, Barry?"

I'm now so glad I didn't say something like, "How's it hanging, Barry?"

The voice on the phone plowed right past my skepticism:

"Son, let me assure you that this *is* Barry Goldwater and it's come to my attention you're writing about defense bases in Arizona and that's something that I take seriously."

Yep – it was Barry Goldwater alright.

We were then writing stories about a commission that was closing military bases around the country. A few years ago I saw this story in a folder and so I may still have it and could check what he said, but the upshot was that he insisted on giving me his version of why the commission should leave the Arizona bases alone. We may have talked for ten or fifteen minutes and then he abruptly thanked me for my time and hung up.

He died on my birthday – May 29, 1998.

After the call, the managing editor walked by my desk and I said, "Steve, Barry Goldwater just called me."

"Oh, sure," he said on his way to his office.

But it really was Barry. Good old, extremist, conservative Barry. He was no George McGovern in my book and man am I glad he never became president.

But I looked up some more information on him and learned that he once entertained the possibility that there really are UFOs coming from other planets.

And so we at least had that in common.

A Couple of Writers I Know
(And I Owe Them Thanks)

Novelist Monique Raphel High is my dear friend. She lives in tony Beverly Hills and I live in less-refined Michigan, and culturally that might seem like two people futilely straining to see each other across the Grand Canyon, but it's not. I know, because when I finally got to meet her, over dinner at The Lobster, a dandy restaurant overlooking the pier in Santa Monica, California, we got uproariously drunk and had a great time. Dinner cost a million dollars and we got there around 7 pm and they tossed us out the door at 1 am. I had Alaskan Salmon, I think, and we depleted their stash of Sauvignon Blanc.

I'm not sure what Monique ate, but I know she had fun and likes Sauvignon Blanc.

Monique was actually my first agent. I came across her purely by chance. Surfing the web somehow took me to a photo of her giving a talk somewhere – LA or New York – and I sensed something even then about her that I knew I'd like. So I e-mailed her, thinking maybe I'd hear back and maybe not, but she replied quickly and said she sensed an immediate connection. In my message I had been blunt: "I'm a new novelist and can use some luck, breaks, and help, and I think you can help me."

After I was awarded a grant by the Elizabeth George Foundation to write my novel *Not Famous Anymore*, I owed much thanks to Monique, who wrote a terrific letter on my behalf. She gave great editing advice on the book and persuaded me to lop off the original first forty pages of the novel because even though they were witty and funny, they didn't offer the best beginning for the story. Since then I have valued being able to cut writing that might be good, but nonetheless not what a story needs.

Monique and I share a love for cats and when my beloved EH died recently, Monique shared my grief. Several years ago she asked me to mail her a picture of EH and it's on her refrigerator. EH would have preened at the notion of having a presence in Beverly Hills.

Monique was born in New York, but was raised in Paris, and is, I believe, technically a baroness. She writes great novels about generations of families. I tend to write about small town people in the middle of choices, though recently I wrote a novel about the last days of Amelia Earhart. Monique was tickled the time I told her my mom in Champaign, Illinois, checked out several of her books from the public library. What better tribute can a writer have?

Go to your local library, folks, and read her books.

I also owe thanks in print to Stuart Dybek, a MacArthur Fellow and currently writer-in-residence at Northwestern University. Stu also supplied a great letter for me when I sought the George Foundation grant. I was in MFA workshops with Stu at Western Michigan University and we still stay in touch by e-mail. My mom sent me a copy of his book, *I Sailed with Magellan*, and it's terrific. It's on the fireplace mantle alongside the ashes of EH and Moonpie – a position of honor. My mom is fond of Stu because when I had my MFA reading at Western Michigan, Stu sat with her and made her feel right at home among a bunch of renegade writers and poets.

During my MFA days, I lived in an old Victorian not far from Stu's house, which sits on a hill by the Kalamazoo College campus. One night pretty late, perhaps near midnight, he called me and said he was at his kitchen table eating pizza and looking at one of my stories and thought it was as good a time as any to talk about it. That was the kind of guy he was back then. Generous as a teacher and writer. Even now, when I e-mail him, I get a prompt reply whether he's in Key West, Prague, or Chicago. When I e-mailed the cover of *Well Deserved* to him in Key West, he replied, "Just got in from spear fishing – great cover." Stu taught me about echoes in fiction – repeated words in the same sentence, for example, that can produce that unwanted echo that draws too much attention to the sentence.

I learned from Monique and Stu and I'm proud to call them friends.

Essential steps in my path as a writer.

Andrew Greeley
(I Met the Priest Who Admired da Bears and Madonna, Too)

Andrew Greeley died the day I wrote this chapter. He was a best-selling novelist and sometimes outspoken Catholic priest. I knew him as a friendly, smiling man generous with his time. Around 1987 he agreed to an interview and invited me to his beautiful Tucson home. He pulled into his driveway just a minute or two after I arrived with a photographer and he apologized profusely for being late because he had been officiating a wedding. It must have been winter because we were able to stand outside without melting.

The first thing I noticed as we filed into Greeley's home through a foyer, was a poster of Jim McMahon, the punky ex-Bears quarterback of '85 Bears fame. The memory of that remarkable team was still fresh and I was happy to hear that Greeley, a Chicagoan who wintered in Tucson, was also a big fan. When we all sat down, I spied another poster – this one of The Material Girl, Madonna. Now, I wish I had met Madonna so I could write a scathing chapter about how desperate for fame she was and how much I found that unappealing, but I'll stop there with the anti-Madonna campaign, and anyway, now I've done the Sullivan Show, as Jim Morrison supposedly said (look it up if you don't know the anecdote) and instead I'll reveal that Greeley admired her, apparently because, like Jim McMahon, she had spirit and was spunky, I suppose.

I can't now recall clearly how he characterized Madonna. I keep wanting to say he used words such as "innocence" and "virginal," which, if true, seem ironic regarding her. But he liked something about her, and after all he was a Bears fan and a Jim McMahon fan, and so I liked him right away. He was entitled to how he really felt about her and my skepticism of her, like my skepticism for The Kardashians (a coming chapter, folks!) is something I'm entitled to feel as well.

I don't have a copy of the Greeley interview anymore, but I do have a copy of one of his novels and he signed it for me. It's there on the fireplace mantle alongside autobiographies signed by Jack Hemingway and John Houseman (another chapter, folks). I can't say Greeley's books are the sort of novels I gravitate to, but I always admired how prolific he was and how he stuck to his guns and wrote them despite the misgivings of his colleagues.

The afternoon at his Tucson house was very pleasant and interesting, and he was quite thoughtful and attentive to the comfort of my photographer and I. Inevitably the interview dug into religious topics, leaving me with the one clear line I recall him saying: "Mormons tend to be a little too strident for me."

I'm not picking on Mormons any more than I would any other cult based on greed and intolerance, but that was what he said when we discussed various faiths. He was just being honest and that's how people should remember him.

But I'll always remember Andrew Greeley as the priest who liked Madonna and Jim McMahon.

John Houseman
(Burly, Crusty Old Prof. Kingsfield!)

I'm a fan of the *Paper Chase* film and later TV series, both starring Academy Award winner John Houseman, a burly and crusty man who I discovered could be somewhat different in real life than his scary, unapproachable Prof. Kingsfield character, which netted him the Oscar. And in *his* autobiography he revealed that the afternoon of the Oscar ceremony he got laid and so that increased my admiration of him.

When I say Houseman was different than Kingsfield, I must point out that he nonetheless shared some characteristics with Kingsfield. I went to a luncheon promoting his autobiography at some impossibly opulent Phoenix hotel, and after he spoke to the audience, in which he certainly looked and sounded like Prof. Kingsfield, he waddled to the back of the room and sat at a table covered with copies of his book and prepared himself for the grueling and gruesome task of pretending to be nice to strangers paying for a few moments of goodwill and an autograph. But if you are a writer, it's nonetheless a good problem to have. It's not as much fun as Ron Jeremy's job, but certainly more dignified.

I noticed that after Houseman went to the back of the room, no one followed him right away and so I seized the opportunity and dashed to the table and introduced myself as a local reporter – and also a *Paper Chase* fan.

I'm not sure which one elicited his subtle sneer, but then again, maybe it was just an autograph signing sneer, or a tic, perhaps, he had barely been aware of.

I asked him how he liked Phoenix and he referred to the drive in from the airport past fast food franchises as "cruising past ptomaine row." Yep – he was still in Kingsfield mode. He even tacked on a reference to once being out in the Arizona desert and getting unexpectedly horned by jumping cholla. That happened to me once, too, in the front yard of my Phoenix house. What was Prof. Kingsfield doing out in the desert? Snorting peyote?

But as Houseman noticed that the audience still had not yet moved in his direction and that it was just one unwashed fan pissing on his shoes instead of a great horde of the unwashed, he lightened up and smiled and even his voice and tone seemed to soften. Now, I had done my homework on the man. As you'll discover in later chapters, Hemingway is a lifelong interest of mine and I knew that when Houseman was a younger man, he had partnered with Orson Wells at the Mercury Theater in New York and had overseen an adaptation of one of Hemingway's Nick Adams stories (*The Battler*, I believe) into a production starring a very young Paul Newman.

I asked Houseman whether he ever met Hemingway and he initially shook his head and brushed aside the notion, but within a short moment caught himself and looked off in the distance for a few seconds and said, "There was a party. In Manhattan somewhere. I don't recall where. But when I walked in, Hemingway was there by the fireplace with a drink in each hand and a woman on each arm."

There's a famous story about how Hemingway and Wells got into a heated shoving match over the narration of *The Spanish Earth*, a film about the Spanish Civil War that Hemingway helped shepherd to success and in which Wells was to have been the narrator but was replaced by an angry Hemingway. I suspect that large men like Hemingway, Wells, and Houseman – large as personalities as well as physically – could not easily be housed for long in the same room, and like lions crowded too close to each other, inevitably giant paws would have to lash out at each other.

On that day in Phoenix in 1986 or 1987, when Houseman had just another year or two to live, he became a gentle, young lion, and found his smile and softer tone for a few minutes with a stranger. But as I left the room, I turned back and I saw Houseman surrounded by a crowd and he was an old lion again, under siege by snapping jackals.

Not So Early Days

Vietnam, a Lake, and a Biker Gang

I spent summers in the 1960s on Lake Mattoon, rich farmland flooded into a decent lake south of Mattoon, Illinois, which has two distinctions, as I recall: Gen. Grant took over his first command in the Civil War in Mattoon, and thanks to Union soldiers Mattoon had a huge outbreak of venereal disease. How's that for a town legacy?

I got laid for the first time on a boat dock with a gal from Mattoon, but unlike all those Union soldiers, I didn't catch anything. And I never met Gen. Grant. He was a couple years older than me and had a war to win. And there was plenty of war going on in the 1960s, too – a culture war in the U.S. and the war far away in the jungles of Vietnam. And I'll even tell you about the time I almost ended up in a war with a biker gang at Lake Mattoon. But more on that later.

This story starts when I was about seventeen. I guess it was 1969, the year of the moon landing, which I still say was staged in a sound studio somewhere, but it's not a conspiracy I especially push, and certainly even less than I push the notion that Yoko Ono broke up the Beatles, or that Gen. Custer actually had a good plan at Little Big Horn. In 1969 I had a year of high school left at Champaign Central High, which produced Olympic champion Bob Richards, but no one else of particular note – including me – that I can recall. But I do recall the moon landing and watching it on TV with a guy named

Steve. A lot of my best adventures seemed to have involved someone named Steve. Anyway, we both worked at the amusement park by the lake that my family owned, which was called, coincidentally enough – Mattoon Beach. There wasn't much of a beach. Just a small strip of sand and a pontoon anchored a few yards from shore. But it was a good place to take a girl swimming because you could duck under the pontoon and make out without being seen from shore. A lot of good feels got copped under that pontoon and I once had sex with a girl from Camargo, Illinois, on the beach at night. Bare butts under the stars. I won't write more about her because she told me her name was Nicole, but later I found out it was really Paula and I was mildly miffed but not entirely sure why.

I have no idea what happened to Steve. Like all the Steves I partnered with in crime, they all seemed to vanish. I can tell you that he was one of those wiry guys with a subtle and dangerous air about him that suggested he could rip your throat out if you crossed him, but he was always nice to me and he was one of the best fishermen on that lake. He had a girlfriend rumored to have posed for Playboy, and she often walked around in a bikini and heels and that was a quite a statement for the Midwest in 1969. Now she makes me think of that line from a Tom Petty song – "She was more than they'd seen."

Anyway, while watching the moon landing, Steve grinned maliciously and said it was likely all a big fake from some desert location or a sound studio and so you now know that I didn't even develop that notion on my own and I recall being a bit shocked he would suggest it. But back then I had not yet learned that Vietnam was a stupid and malicious mistake and that the government could not be trusted and that John Wayne was not real and instead a fake and conservative zealot who forgot he was just an actor. Maybe more on John Wayne later.

Life at Mattoon Beach during those 1960s summers was pretty nice for a kid with no more ambition than to chase girls, drink beer, listen to the Beatles and Rolling Stones and smoke marijuana, and believe me – I qualified. I worked with a bunch of guys a couple years older and already in college over at Eastern Illinois University in Charleston – which I would flunk out of a few years later because I spent more time at keggers than classes, but perhaps that's a future chapter. We were the amusement park 'limberdicks', which is a pretty Midwestern word that basically means something along the lines of blue collar worker but with an added dose of redneck.

At that amusement park, I learned how to operate a Ferris Wheel, Bumper Cars, A Tilt-A-Whirl, and a miniature passenger train that had several miles of tracks and often derailed. It's a wonder no one ever got killed – either us or park patrons – because we basically drank beer and smoked joints all day and night while we worked. Yes – we operated heavy machinery while drunk and stoned. Don't try stuff like that at home folks, because we were *professional* drunks and stoners. Late at night, when the park was closed, we'd drink more beer and smoke more dope and sometimes we'd take turns hanging from the bottom of a Tilt-A-Whirl seat as it went round and round.

At some point, I began to meet a few veterans returning from Vietnam. The closest town to the lake was Neoga, just a few miles up the road, and Neoga townies often partied with us at the beach. Some of the townies brought out a couple of guys who'd come home on leave. We all got drunk together and, to me, Vietnam did not seem very real and they didn't talk about it that much. It wasn't long after that that one of them came back from Vietnam escorting the body of the other one. That was when Vietnam started to become real to me. It was no longer helicopters landing in rice paddies on TV. From then on in those days Vietnam was this ominous presence, a sort of shadow that one could not ever quite escape.

Remember that biker gang I mentioned? Well, first off, they weren't the Hell's Angels or anything like that. They were local dickheads on Harleys who thought they were tough and who certainly were probably tougher than me or the guys I worked with. Muscle-bound guys in leather. I remember that several of them claimed to have guns and most had knives on their hips. I didn't ask to see the guns. When they looked at us, we tried not to stare. We could just tell they were guys who didn't think twice about starting and finishing a fight. It was in their eyes – an absence of fear and a comfortable disregard for consequences in the way they stared past people, through people. They weren't guys destined to grow up and become bank presidents or sell insurance.

Inevitably, as the bikers got drunker, they misbehaved and jostled park patrons and started pawing girls. I guess there was a confrontation, but there were a lot of people around – too many for guys who prefer to do their dirty deeds when they outnumber their foes, and so after much staring and finger-pointing they left, but vowed to come back when the park was closed in a few hours.

They weren't kidding. After the park emptied and the main gate was chained shut for the night, we were sitting around by the park restaurant eating hamburgers and hot dogs and guzzling beer. From where we sat you could look at the long causeway road that stretched about a mile across the lake. We heard them first, the sound of motors being revved, and then we saw their lights as they came around the bend on the far side of the lake. We watched them slowly rumble across the causeway road toward us. The lake and amusement park were out in the middle of the country. There was no town and only a few houses along the lake. No place to run to.

The bikers pulled up to the main gate and revved their bikes and took turns laying rubber up and down the road by the gate. We had slipped around behind the restaurant where there was a small bathroom building and we hid behind it and could peek around it and see the bikers on the other side of the gate. The bikers yelled creative and colorful insults that had a lot to do with our mothers. They shook the gate and rattled the chain. And they yelled that they'd be coming in to get us. I was still too young to be properly scared right away, but pretty quickly I got the idea that things could get pretty dangerous. A couple of the guys I worked with retrieved a shotgun and a rifle from the restaurant. Someone handed me a .22 pistol. And I remember that one guy grabbed a baseball bat.

There we were, taking positions behind the bathroom building, and it dawned on me that it wasn't so different than being a soldier in Vietnam. Less firepower, to be sure, and we weren't going to be able to call in a napalm air strike to see us through, but nonetheless it was armed men against armed men. I don't recall just how long we hunched over in our positions, hefting weapons. I pointed my pistol at the gate and waited. I'm sure the whole thing took far less than we thought at the time. But at the time it felt like hours and sweat trickled down my forehead.

There was a point at which we were sure they were coming and the guy with the shotgun next to me injected a shell into the chamber and that sound gave me a chill. It was loud and snarly and we all knew that the bikers heard it, too, and they took notice. They sat there at the gate, astride their bikes, and stared. They knew we were there because we had not been careful enough to stay hidden. We were just limberdick kids, really, with guns, facing guys not much older but far harder than we were and the possibility for things getting out of hand seemed to grow each second. I had pointed my pistol for so long that my arm was tired, but I didn't dare lower it.

And then abruptly it was over. Like air suddenly fleeing a tire. The bikers lost their desire for a gun battle, or maybe they just got bored, or thought of something else to do that would be easier and more fun, and one by one they revved their bikes and roared back across the causeway road and disappeared around the bend on the road into Neoga.

We held our positions for a while, not sure if it was a trick. I stared across that lake for a long time, expecting to suddenly see motorcycle lights as they made their charge to try and finish us. But they never came back and I don't recall ever seeing them again. They were the possibility of disaster averted for reasons we'd never know.

And after a while, we grabbed more beers and drank them on the beach watching the moonlight dance on the water, and we didn't think much about what had happened at all.

We were young.

Very young.

We Weren't Soldiers

John Wayne's teeth! John Wayne's teeth!
Are they plastic? Are they steel?
–Song from *Smoke Signals*

Around 1972 or so, I flunked out of Eastern Illinois University because attending classes interfered with my hobby of chasing girls and swilling beer. I remember running into one of my professors on campus and he said, "Hey, I've been wanting to talk to you."

I said, "Cool. What did you want to talk about?"

"I wanted to tell you you're flunking my class."

"Shit," I said, "I already knew that."

My GPA had dipped slightly below 2.0 and it was miraculous it had not fallen even more. I heard I might have petitioned to stay in school and improve my GPA, but I felt instead that I was done with school for the time being and so I went back home to try and figure out what came next. Well, the first thing that came next was a change in my draft status from 2S, a student deferment, to 1A, which meant I was a prime candidate for the Army. And my draft lottery number was 62, I think, which was piss-poor low.

Soon a letter from President Nixon arrived and informed me I was being invited to serve my country and the first step was a physical in Chicago. And so I made the very wise and mature decision to guzzle beer all night in bars on the University of Illinois campus along with two guys I went to high school with who had also been called up for physicals. We lurched drunkenly aboard a bus at the downtown Champaign Greyhound station around three or four in the morning for the ride to Chicago, which we would not remember because we passed out.

In Chicago, several Army sergeants herded us and our monumental hangovers off the bus like we were cattle, and we found ourselves in a room to take a written test. I thought, what the hell do you have to know to get in the Army? I have no memory of what was on that test. I do remember that as the sergeants handed out pencils, a boy with blonde hair a lot like Gregg Allman's produced a harmonica and started playing and everyone stopped working to listen – except the sergeants, who plucked the guy out of his chair like he was garbage in a bag and carted him away. We never saw that guy again.

After the exam we spent hours in long lines – either naked or in our underpants, and I honestly don't recall which it was, and at some point we all carried our own urine in specimen jars and guys joked it would be a bad time to suddenly get a hard on, but I was too hung over for that. By the end of the day a doctor examined my elbow – the one I broke so badly as a kid – and he said my surgery qualified as corrective bone surgery and the Army had a rule against drafting guys with that unless it was a national emergency and Vietnam wasn't. Just a national disgrace, I would later realize.

"Congratulations," the doctor said and just like that I had gone from 1A to 4F – unfit to serve, which is ironic because I could always shoot a rifle pretty well.

Being 4F had a bit of a stigma to it – like you weren't really a man, for example, if you couldn't be a soldier. In those days, as Philip Caputo wrote about so well in *A Rumor of War*, I still had a romantic notion about the glory of war and being a soldier. All I knew about war was the John Wayne propaganda in "The Fighting Seabees" and "The Sands of Iwo Jima." Only years later, for example, did I learn that Wayne never actually served his country and was much happier to pretend he did. Other actors actually served – Clark Gable flew combat missions over Germany, for example.

We weren't soldiers, my friends and I, but I guess we were resigned to going if we were called. It didn't occur to me to flee to Canada or Sweden or become a conscious objector, though now I know, as novelist/Vietnam vet Tim O'Brien knew, that the guys who left or claimed objections were the truly brave ones.

I remember being in my mid-thirties, when I was a reporter in Arizona, and seeing *Platoon* when it came out in theaters. It was a stunning film. It made Vietnam seem real and not rather cartoonish like John Wayne films. After it was over, I stood outside the theater, sort of reflecting on what I had just seen, and I noticed several men slightly older than me come out of the theater with tears streaming down their cheeks. I knew they must be Vietnam veterans and for the first time had seen a film about Vietnam that was very authentic and it had brought back all their memories and emotions. They may have even felt they saw themselves on the screen.

I knew a guy in my Phoenix apartment complex who served aboard helicopters in Vietnam. He told me that one day as they approached a landing zone, he saw what he thought were large white boulders on the ground, but they were instead the naked bodies of dead American soldiers. Those images were burned into his brain and one night he freaked out at the apartment complex as Vietnam came rushing back into him in full color, and it took three of us to subdue him and take him to a hospital.

Even though I never served in the military, Vietnam was my war, too. I knew someone who died there and I knew others who had come back from it. During the war years Vietnam was a constant presence, like someone standing a bit too close behind you. How the war was prosecuted and represented by the government colored our evolving views of our government in those days. I learned not to believe in John Wayne anymore and not to blindly trust the government. Because of that I'm connected to the Vietnam War, too, in my own way.

Bloodlessly, but connected.

Saving Democracy
(Why Conservativism is the Worst Ism We Face)

In *Wall Street* Gordon Gekko famously says, "Greed is good." And in the sequel after a stint in prison, he discovers that greed has become pretty much standard operating procedure. But it's not just greed that is ruining America and threatening democracy, though greed certainly is front and center in the process.

The real threat, as economist Paul Krugman has pointed out, is that the Republican Party is controlled by extremist whack jobs that are stupid, intolerant, incompetent, and don't believe in democracy: The Koch Brothers, Rush Limbaugh, Sean Hannity, Michelle Bachman, Sarah Palin, Grover Norquist, and Tea Party retards in Congress. John Boehner and Mitch McConnell, too.

Now, we've had some other isms in this country – communism, fascism, discoism, Bieberism – but they have been mostly irrelevant. American Nazis and communists are always a bit of a joke. Disco died quickly, thank God, and I'm not sure who this Bieber fellow is or what makes him worthy of fame and wealth – and teenage squeals – but I am confident he is not The Beatles and will fade and one day be irrelevant and merely a judge on American Idol. You know, sort of like Steven Tyler from Aerosmith.

I agree with Krugman that this last election exposed the conservative movement as morally bankrupt and its ideas as nothing more than selfishness and intolerance and in some cases, seriously delusional and just plain incorrect. But Krugman is also accurate in reminding us that since the GOP still controls the House, they are like a wounded lion that can still rip our faces off. And so we must finish them off. Because a true democracy has no room for GOPism. The folks who say we need a sane Republican Party as part of a two-party system mean well, but they are wrong. We don't need people who would step on their mothers' graves to serve the rich at the expense of everyone else.

And that's who the GOP now is – the party of two percent of America (I stole that from Krugman). We saw that Mitt Romney would truly say anything to try and be president and help the rich be richer, the poor be poorer, the middle class more endangered. Facts? Irrelevant. His campaign people famously issued a statement declaring that the campaign would not be affected by fact checking – essentially, facts didn't matter to them, as TV commentator Chris Matthews so bluntly put it.

Conservative columnist Jonah Goldberg claims that the political process is rigged against conservatives, that somehow Americans say they want politicians with convictions, but punish conservatives who demonstrate their convictions.

No, no, no!

And once more, Jonah – *no!*

Voters aren't punishing conservatives because they have convictions.

They punish conservatives because they ought to be convicted for some of their wacko convictions.

It's not how the GOP delivers its message – *it's the message!*

Folks – Hitler had convictions.

So did Stalin.

And even Genghis Khan, I suppose.

But that doesn't mean they should ever have been allowed to run countries.

Anyone who claims that cutting taxes on the rich creates jobs isn't misunderstood.

They're lying.

And just plain wrong.

Cutting taxes on the rich has never been shown to create jobs.

Cutting taxes on the rich creates an extra Jacuzzi in their McMansions.

Why does GOPism insist on claiming tax cuts create jobs?

Because they need to say something to disguise their disinformation campaign and they don't have an actual factual explanation for their obsessive need to take warm showers with their rich masters. They have become Chatty-Kathy dolls: pull the string and they keep bleating, "Save the rich! Save the rich!"

Face it, folks, GOPism is just selfishness. Intolerance. And fiscal baboonery.

They hate gays.

They hate women.

They hate Europeans.

Brown and black people annoy and offend them and they wish they'd all just disappear.

They hate facts.

They hate reality.

But if the GOP is mostly counting on white male votes, as evidenced in the last presidential election, soon they will be the ones to disappear.

Good riddance.

Or, we could speed up the process. Since the president has been re-elected and we narrowly averted becoming the United States of Bain Capital, the nuttier of the conservative nutcases among us in primitive regions such as Texas and Oklahoma have signed petitions calling for their states to secede.

Political pundits call it frustrated posturing.

Call it what you like, but by all means – let them go. Now.

Don't let the door hit you on the ass.

I say the government should even provide the ships to speed these disgruntled conservatives far from our shores and the democracy they hate so much.

Let them go find a little country of their own.

A little banana republic they can turn into fundamentalist heaven.

Bless their little pointy heads.

On Writing and Teaching

Novels

"Great literature is simply language charged with meaning to the utmost possible degree."
–Ezra Pound

Pound got it right, even though he eventually went a little crazy. In order to illustrate what he succinctly defined, humor me a bit because to talk about great novels, I first need to talk about great rock albums: When I chat about the great albums, the task is easy: I start with *Sergeant Pepper's Lonely Hearts Club Band* by The Beatles, *Pet Sounds* by The Beach Boys, *Exile on Main Street* by the Rolling Stones, and from there I make a list I like. Many of the reputable lists agree, at least, on which albums belong at the top or near it. It's like that with movies, too: many critics coronate *Citizen Kane* and *Casablanca* as the best (though I say it's *Lawrence of Arabia*).

But novels? Opinions vary – wildly!

Groucho Marx: "From the moment I picked up your book until I laid it down I was convulsed with laughter. Someday I intend reading it."

Or Woody Allen: "I took a speed reading course and read *War and Peace* in twenty minutes. It involves Russia."

So, which novels are the greatest? Well, the short answer is this: a whole bunch of them, to be sure. I can't really explain why plenty of folks seem to agree that

Sergeant Pepper is the greatest rock album and yet far fewer people can agree on designating one top novel. Or even what the top twenty should contain. The top 100 or 200? That's a little easier. But how do we establish a ranking? Can we?

Is *Ulysses* by James Joyce the greatest of novels? It certainly gets mentioned often, but even though I admire Joyce's creative genius, I still find *Ulysses* rather unreadable, which will certainly set me apart as some sort of Neanderthal to some scholars. But that's just my view. Personally, I admire Joyce's *Dubliners* much more than his novels. I might even be tempted to tab it as number one if we were ranking story collections. It does seem like the *Sergeant Pepper* of story collections.

When were the great novels written? A while ago – another short answer. I feel strongly that a novel must endure for many years and stand the test of time before being called great. Wine and literature share that requirement. In the last twenty years or so there have been terrific novels written – and if they really are terrific, let them marinate and ferment some more before promotion to the elite lists. The focus here will tend toward works created at the end of the 19th Century and well into the 20th Century and generally before 1990 – another arbitrary decision. They have stood the test of time and have not faded away. Let the novels after 1990 become another and future tidal wave of greatness and someone else can pick and choose from among them as I am doing here now.

Hemingway said it well: "First, one must endure."

Here are some novels, then – and *not* in order of rank – that get bandied about when people discuss the great ones, and it's just one tiny sliver of bark off the towering tree of literature:

- *The Great Gatsby* by F. Scott Fitzgerald

- *The Sun Also Rises* by Ernest Hemingway
- *The Sound and the Fury* by William Faulkner
- *To the Lighthouse* by Virginia Woolf
- *The Heart is a Lonely Hunter* by Carson McCullers
- *The Age of Innocence* by Edith Wharton
- *Pride and Prejudice* by Jane Austen
- *Beloved* by Toni Morrison
- *The Catcher in the Rye* by J.D. Salinger
- *Catch-22* by Joseph Heller
- *The Color Purple* by Alice Walker
- *The Grapes of Wrath* by John Steinbeck

Notice anything about the list? It's equally balanced between men and women. That was the criteria I arbitrarily decided to base it on. And all are great novels, to be sure. Not a one diminishes the overall quality of the list, though quickly someone might shriek – but where are the novels of Vladimir Nabokov and Joseph Conrad? What about Ayn Rand and Willa Cather and Margaret Atwood and William Kennedy? I love Kennedy's *Ironweed,* for example. And Evan Connell – his *Mr. Bridge* and *Mrs. Bridge* are terrific novels. What about Erskine Caldwell? I met Caldwell and interviewed him in Arizona shortly before his death. Should I be influenced to toss his *Tobacco Road* onto the list as a result? I easily could have added him or any of the others to the list, but I made choices based on the severe restrictions of space necessitating a very small sampling. I forced myself to omit selections I love every bit as much as what I kept. Now we begin to realize the difficulty – impossibility, perhaps – of designating a ranking system for novels (which somehow seems a bit easier for rock and roll) when we realize the list above includes novels I really love and some I don't, which tells me that lists like these will always be inherently flawed. They are more wish lists than anything that can be definitive.

It's a matter of taste, then. I love the timeless love story Austen tells in *Pride and Prejudice*. I love the comic absurdity that's evident in Heller's classic *Catch-22*. I love the richness and complexities of life and intricacies of human character, conveyed in very different styles, by Hemingway and Fitzgerald. I'm less enamored (though impressed by the storytelling ability) with Wharton's work. That goes for McCullers, too – impressive, but not entirely my cup of tea. Faulkner's skills always leave me in awe (like with Joyce) and yet I sometimes find his stories too dense. And while *The Sound and the Fury* is often mentioned first when it comes to Faulkner, I much prefer *As I Lay Dying*.

A matter of taste.

So, far from assembling above a short list of the greatest, I instead assembled a short list of indisputably great novels mindful of the emphasis I wanted on gender balance. To me it just underscores my belief that a definitive greatest novels list is impossible to do. Certainly restricting a list to twelve is absurd. Or even fifty. A list of 100, to me, would just be a starting point. Two hundred would not be too many. So, instead of worrying about where novels rank on a list, which is pretty much a matter of taste and preference, let's instead shift the focus to recognizing the great many novels that belong on an ever growing list of great novels and leave ranking to college basketball and football polls.

Before novels can be ranked, there's the process of deciding which ones are good enough to even *be* ranked. Sort of like a cover charge to get into a bar and hear the band. And it seems to me to be a much more complicated process than the one that determines *Sergeant Pepper* is timeless and incredible and innovative and ground-breaking – you *hear* all that the first time you listen to it. Waves of music wash over you and you truly understand why there will never again be a group quite like The Beatles. The staggering genius of *Sergeant Pepper* is clear and immediate from the very first cut and is resoundingly reiterated with that last and lingering chord that haunts the end of *A Day in the Life.*

A rock album can be evaluated in an hour. But novels often pull us in for days or weeks before the creative journey is complete and we have reached a final perspective on what we experienced. And we must feel we have experienced something. I expect a great novel's first page to be a door that swings open for me to slip inside the story effortlessly, seamlessly, and immediately connecting me to a conflict. Hemingway does that with the cadence of that first elegant and rhythmic sentence of *The Old Man and the Sea*:

'He was an old man who fished alone in a skiff in the Gulf Stream and he had gone eighty-four days now without taking a fish.'

In just twenty-seven words the reader has collided with mortality – '*an old man*' – great loneliness – '*alone in a skiff*' – and great failure – '*eighty-four days now without taking a fish.*'

And *the Gulf Stream* signals that the opening takes place on a large and dangerous and unpredictable stage.

Plenty of drama, to be sure. From that brilliant opening, the reader becomes a fellow traveler with Santiago the fisherman. We feel the sun and the sting of the salt spray and we endure, too, the great pain of failure and despair. Our emotions are cleaved open.

The opening of A Tale of Two Cities is also one of the best and most well-known in the English language, even though it might flunk a composition course because it's a series of comma splices – a very skillful series:

'It was the best of times, it was the worst of times, it was the age of wisdom, it was the age of foolishness, it was the epoch of belief, it was the epoch of incredulity, it was the season of Light, it was the season of Darkness, it was the spring of hope, it was the winter of despair, we had everything before us, we had nothing before us, we were all going direct to Heaven, we were all going direct the other way--in short, the period was so far like the present period, that some of its noisiest authorities insisted on its being received, for good or for evil, in the superlative degree of comparison only.'

Wow – what an amazing and wonderful whirlwind of contradictions!

The ending, too, of A Tale of Two Cities is famous and memorable. There Sydney Carton goes to his death by guillotine but first utters these immortal words:

'It is a far, far better thing that I do, than I have ever done; it is a far, far better rest that I go to than I have ever known.'

Magnificent writing.

Endings, then, are as important as beginnings when judging a novel's greatness. Hemingway claimed to have re-worked the ending of A Farewell to Arms many times before completing the scene where Frederic Henry sadly but stoically moves on after Catherine Barkley has died during childbirth:

'After a while I went out and left the hospital and walked back to the hotel in the rain.'

In that short and simple sentence, we nonetheless feel his great pain and resignation and loneliness.

Hemingway: "All good books are alike in that they are truer than if they had really happened and after you are finished reading one you will feel that all that happened to you and afterwards it all belongs to you; the good and the bad, the ecstasy, the remorse."

Edith Wharton: "A classic is classic not because it conforms to certain structural rules, or fits certain definitions (of which its author had quite probably never heard). It is classic because of a certain eternal and irrepressible freshness."

A great novel, then, is a destination with a universe of experiences we can't forget. They become our experiences, too. An out of body experience: our hands hold the book but our minds – our souls – have entered it and we skip along on the pages beside the characters and see the sweat bead on their foreheads and watch their hands tremble and hear their voices quiver and when it rains, we feel the drops hitting our heads, too.

A great novel reflects and reveals the human condition – it reflects a society but also exposes it. Dickens did that so very well in *A Tale of Two Cities*. So did Austen in *Pride and Prejudice*, where we negotiate the minefields of love and class distinctions alongside Lizzie Bennett and Mr. Darcy.

A great novel is populated by great characters – memorable characters:

• Jake Barnes in *The Sun Also Rises:* resigned and sad and quietly desperate in the eye of a hurricane of lost souls.

• Yossarian in *Catch-22:* afraid and confused and justifiably paranoid and yet also hopeful to survive a war that makes no sense to him.

• Holden Caulfield in *The Catcher in the Rye:* already jaded and cynical at age sixteen. What bothers him most, the world around him or the world inside him?

• Elizabeth Bennett in *Pride and Prejudice:* certainly one of the most beloved heroines in literature. She is playful and lively and smart and stands her ground with Lady Catherine de Bourgh. Eventually Mr. Darcy realizes class barriers can't prevent him from loving her.

• Celie in *The Color Purple:* an odyssey from poverty and abuse that culminates in self-confidence and happiness.

Character Counts

What's a novel without characters – without people? It would be what I think of as a lot of postmodern mood, some description, a pretentious attempt to create something where there really is nothing. It's all surface and no depth. Now, non-human things – landscape and geography – can become characters in a story, to be sure. The Gulf Stream and fish are characters in *The Old Man and the Sea*. A town can be a character in a story. I was quite happy when a review of my novel *Well Deserved* referred to the setting, tiny Argus, Illinois, as a character in its own right. I certainly intended that.

But people make a story work.

So make us care about the people in your novel. And make them real and not cardboard cutouts. Show us them living their actual lives and saying the things they'd really say using the real words they would use. Avoid having them make speeches and instead have them converse – have them *talk* to each other as though they were sitting in your living room. If they are profane people, have them cuss. If they're stridently religious, show us how they struggle with their faith or how it helps them through a day. Show us their good sides and bad sides. Give us their inner thoughts no matter how small-minded or noble.

Make us care.

Make us see them as human, like us.

Show and don't tell – more of that sage old advice that still matters.

That said, though, it can be hard to sustain a character over several hundred pages. But if you make people like your character – or at least want to understand your character – then readers will enjoy the ride as you take characters through their lives and toward some inevitable resolution of a conflict. Think again of that opening sentence from *The Old Man and the Sea:*

'He was an old man who fished alone in a skiff in the Gulf Stream and he had gone eighty-four days now without taking a fish.'

Santiago is basically an aging and lonely human dot floating alone in the immense blue Gulf Stream with failure ever present on his mind for eighty-four days now. How can we not have sympathy for him? We feel his despair, his loneliness and so we will read further. We want to know – we *need* to know – how Santiago's luck will play out.

I say put your character or characters into conflict from the very start of your novel. If not with the first sentence, then surely by the end of the first paragraph – hook the reader as solidly as Santiago hoped to hook a marlin.

Here's the opening line from Ayn Rand's *The Fountainhead:*

'Howard Roark laughed.'

Simple – but human. A person doing something human. Being human.

Once readers see that characters are human, with emotions and fears and desires and hopes and dreams and failures and successes, they can begin to visualize them and suspend their disbelief – accept the characters as not words on a flat page in a book, but people with dimensions that they can see and hear and care about.

We know characters by what they say and do. How they speak to others and how they behave toward other characters reveals a character's – *character*.

Character can also be revealed by what isn't said and by what isn't done. If a character withholds information from another character, what does that say about the first character? It could signal that he or she is dishonest or mean, for example. But if a character in a novel reveals useful information to another character, we sense honesty, compassion, loyalty.

Dialogue
Characters need to speak!

After all, you want readers to think of your characters as living people. And a novel that is only narration quickly becomes deadly dull and is then telling rather than showing, and it doesn't allow characters to spring to life – to speak for themselves. Dialogue is indeed a form of showing because when characters speak, they are demonstrating their views and attitudes. Instead of being told something – we hear it. Get used to the idea that a novel is an ongoing conversation and relationship with readers. We may initially assimilate the novel by *reading* it, but we are also *hearing* it in our heads and ultimately *seeing* it with the little mental camera we all have in our minds.

Writing dialogue is not easy. A writer must avoid having characters give sermons, for example – unless the character is a minister standing at a pulpit, of course. And writers must avoid what I call informational dialogue. That's dialogue that sounds more like a database than a real person having a real conversation with another character. For example:

"How's your wife?" Jim said.

"Carol? My short but pretty blond wife who I met in Biloxi and married fifteen years ago?" Bill said.

Ouch! *Instead:*

"How's your wife?" Jim said.

"Carol's fine," Bill said. "She got a promotion at work."

"Really? That's great." Jim nodded and after a pause said, "How long have you two been married?"

Bill smiled and looked away for moment. "I guess it's fifteen years now. Hard to believe."

"Where'd you two meet?" Jim said.

"Biloxi, Mississippi. I'd just gotten out of the Army and she was a waitress at a place called Shorty's. I thought she was the prettiest blond I'd ever seen."

Use name tags – 'he said' and 'she said' – but don't overdo it. Use them in places during a conversation between characters to help keep readers clued as to who is speaking, but don't allow name tags to be too intrusive. You can resist a name tag in places where it's clear who spoke the line and who speaks next. Obviously this is easier when there are no more than two characters in a conversation.

And remember that 'he said' and 'she said' work just fine. Don't try to exhaust the possibilities. It needn't be a competition to see how many different name tags can be used. That would just draw attention to the tags, which ought to basically be silent partners in recording dialogue and identifying speakers. Imagine how distracting it could get:

"I'm so psyched," Todd ejaculated.

"I hear you, man," Bill regurgitated.

Hemingway claimed to be a good listener and that it helped him develop his ear for dialogue. Listen to people everywhere – really listen and hear what they say and how they say it. The conversations you hear around you while you wait for a plane at an airport gate – those conversations reveal how people really talk to each other. Do you ride a bus to get somewhere? Listen to what people are saying. A coffee shop should be an excellent place for listening. You don't want your characters to sound like they're giving speeches. You want them to sound like the folks at the coffee shop.

What Should You Write About?

Here's another short answer: write about what you know. That's old and sage advice that has been passed along for many years from writer to writer, from teacher to student. My very first fiction writing teacher, Daniel Curley at the University of Illinois, was the first one to tell me that. He also passed along advice that I think comes originally from Flannery O' Connor: sit at your machine. Actually, that's been among the best advice I have ever been given because a novel gets done by doing the work and doing it daily. It's an art, but also a job and it happens by committing to regular work.

But do you really have to always write about something you know or have seen? Writing about something you have experienced certainly has advantages – you have seen the conditions firsthand that your characters will also endure. You know the landscape, literally, of the story you will tell. But when Stephen Crane wrote about the Civil War in his novel *The Red Badge of Courage*, he had not been to that war and did not know it, so to speak. And Michael Shaara had not experienced the Civil War, either, in his terrific 1974 novel *The Killer Angels*. But it won the 1975 Pulitzer Prize for Fiction.

The notion, then, that you write about what you know has obvious limitations. And after all, it's fiction – it's made up. It didn't really happen unless it's a historical novel, for example, where reality and fiction are mingled to tell a story. That's what Shaara does so brilliantly with *The Killer Angels*: he takes us through some true and accurate events of the Civil War along with Lee and Grant and Chamberlain and Longstreet, but much of the story is fictionalized.

My best short story, *Little Man*, owes its genesis to something my grandmother once said that rolled around in my head for years until it sparked the creation of a fictional couple and the story of their deteriorating marriage. My grandmother's line is even in the story as a snippet of dialogue, but all the rest is made up.

Sometimes what you know is just a starting point and that's all it needs to be.

So, You Want to Write a Novel

What *is* a novel? It's a very long story that can span a thousand years or just a day.

It can explore the conflicts of just one person or many people – a society, for example.

Why write one? Novelists, in my experience, tend to have little choice but to write – to share the stories in their heads. It's not a hobby and instead borders much closer to obsession. I've written ten novels and when I am writing, I recognize it's a need. It's something I *have* to do because like other novelists, my ego apparently requires me to believe I have something to say and that other people should listen.

Hemingway: "There is nothing to writing. All you do is sit down at a typewriter and bleed."

Toni Morrison: "If there's a book you really want to read, but it hasn't been written yet, then you must write it."

Writing a novel is very hard work and I always suggest that it become a daily task until finished so that you don't lose sight of your story. And I do strenuously suggest that you have an actual story to tell. Something should *happen*. Someone should *change* or *learn* – or *not learn* and be perhaps doomed to the same tragic mistakes over and over.

Tell a story instead of merely showing off your vocabulary or writing style. Too often contemporary novels are more concerned with mood or a prose style and they leave out a story. Nothing *happens*. But, gee, the words sure are pretty to look at.

Words aren't merely to be cast on paper like diamonds embedded in black velvet at a jeweler, though it's true that the right words shine like diamonds. But words have work to do. Be a *storyteller*. Tell a good story using words that are specific and clear and vivid when they need to be vivid, and style takes care of itself. Novels that are all style and no story won't endure. And they shouldn't.

Don't try to write like Hemingway or Joyce or Austen or any of the many others. Read their work to see how a story can be told, but write your own story and develop your own *voice*. When you discover your voice – your own unique diction and word choice and use – you will also have discovered your style.

Voice is important and it's part of form. The form you choose for telling your story will help determine the writing voice you employ. This necessitates an examination of the elements of fiction, such as plot – a sequence of events that carry your story along. Without a plot, a story is somewhat like a car without a motor: it might look good sitting there, but it isn't going anywhere.

When it comes to fiction elements, I like how novelist Madison Smartt Bell expresses it in his book *Narrative Design: A Writer's Guide to Structure:*

"Suppose that the elemental ingredients of fiction may be grouped in one or another of four major categories: plot, character, tone, and form. To define these terms quickly and simply: plot is what happens in a narrative; character is who it happens to (or who makes it happen); and tone is what it sounds like. Form is the pattern of its assembly, its arrangement, structure and design."

Bell explains that a writer ought to have a tangible sense of how the novel will achieve form and be structured before the story gets started. The form decisions a writer makes will affect the story itself and how it gets told. That's essentially what form does in this context – it packages your story and determines how best to tell it. And that's crucial.

Will it work best to tell the story in first person, through the eyes of a primary character? Or will that be too limited a view and thus third person, through the eyes of multiple characters, is the way to go? That's one of the first decisions I always make before I start writing a novel. I have my idea, which can be as thin as a bit of conversation, an opening line, a scene with an obvious conflict, who someone is and how they live etc., but before I can pursue it I need to know *how* I am going to tell the story.

When I wrote my novel *Well Deserved*, all I had at first was the name of a character, Jessie Archer, and where he lived and what he did: he sold pot from a trailer in woods by a lake just outside a small Illinois town. So I wrote the first chapter and thought initially it might be a first person novel through Jessie's eyes. But I quickly felt the limits of that point of view for the story I wanted to tell, which I knew was going to feature other characters as strong and multi-dimensional as Jessie. By the end of the first chapter, I had a second character, Dominick, not just entering the story, but entering Jessie's universe and becoming an equal as a character. And so I understood then that I wanted multiple narrators with equal narrative weights because in many cases, how a scene unfolded to one character would be viewed in the next chapter by another character and of course some details of their perspective on the shared events could vary. First person was not the best choice for me because as *Well Deserved* quickly evolved, it became the story of four characters – Jessie, Dominick, Art, and Nicole – of pretty much equal narrative weight and importance whose lives are entwined and whose futures depend to varying degrees on a shared event. They all needed their time on stage, I concluded, hence the choice of multiple narrators taking turns telling the story – but also *advancing* the story.

With the novel's form established, I was then able to take off quite nicely with multiple narrators constantly tossing shared events back and forth and furthering the story toward its eventual conclusions. Establishing the most effective form package for my story made it easier to *tell* the story. Indeed, it made it *possible* to tell the story.

But when I wrote the *Well Deserved* sequel, called *The Last Stop*, which takes place ten years after *Well Deserved*, I faced a different situation. *The Last Stop* is about one of the primary characters from *Well Deserved*, Art Millage, and so first person was the way to go. For that story, first person was not limiting and thus the correct choice for form.

Teaching and Cell Phones

I once called a girlfriend in Champaign, Illinois, from a gas station pay phone in Jonesboro, Arkansas, using enough coins to seed a wishing well. Patience – I'm working my way to a story about teaching.

It was 1965, when I was in junior high school, The Beatles and Rolling Stones creating the soundtrack of my life, and I had snuck down to the station from my grandparents' house a block away. I don't recall what I talked about with my girlfriend that day. We could barely hear each other. I do remember that the process was like reaching someone on another planet, but in those days that's how it was.

We accepted it.

It wasn't tragic and it didn't seem strange.

It was what it was – life.

Back at our house in Champaign, the family telephone clung to a wall in the kitchen. I think it was yellow. And touch tone. The phone had a very long cord – so long it could stretch and wind around the doorway and up the living room stairs to the hallway to the bedrooms. That was what passed for privacy. If I wanted to make smoochy talk with my girlfriend – a skinny peroxide-blonde named Linda – it was either from the bedroom hallway or the cool and dimly-lit basement.

Time on a phone back then was often related directly to how many coins you had in your pocket or how often family members stepped over you while you whispered what foolish teenagers whisper in a hallway about true love, or who liked Paul or Ringo best. Just for the record – early on I was a Keith Richards fan (I even listened to *Let It Bleed* and *Beggar's Banquet* while writing this).

Now, fast forward to today. Keith Richards is somehow still alive, though it always seems best that someone should kick him or check his pulse periodically to make sure. And now I teach college English and I'm a novelist (rock and roll didn't rot my brain after all!). I don't know what happened to Linda, who ceased to be my girlfriend some time during the Johnson Administration. I can't recall whether it was Paul or Ringo for her. And time and access are no longer in short supply when it comes to talking on a phone – on a *cell* phone.

But now I often wish that time was indeed in shorter supply for today's phone users. I also wish the debate was still about Paul and Ringo instead of the Kardashians or Justin Bieber, but that's altogether another story. You see, in the developmental English courses I teach, for example, my students read Eric A. Taub's excellent essay 'Cell Yell: Thanks for (Not) Sharing' about the curious and annoying habit many people have of constantly yelling into their cell phones no matter where they are – profanity optional but certainly common.

The week we spend on Taub's essay is always interesting to me, but a bit funny – hypocritical? – because few students will admit to cell yell. From the comments they post in class, it always seems something other people do – their crazy uncle, for example. Or a friend they aren't quite sure they actually like. My chief concern, though, is not so much that people yell into their cell phones, but that they seem to use them so often that talk really and truly does become cheap.

And by extension, writing skills are eroded, I believe. Think about it: growing up without cell phones, people of my generation had to learn how to communicate effectively, directly, and in a short amount of time. When I called Linda from Arkansas I only had a couple minutes and so the focus had to be on expressing *true love* instead of the minutiae of the day.

But, minutiae are what it's all about now. Millions of people daily spend hours on their cell phones spewing thousands of words, but saying very little of importance. Who do we need to talk to all day? Well, certainly pizza delivery for one.

But, after pizza, how many emergencies are there every day? I have seen people talk by cell phone while standing in the same hallway after concluding a face-to-face conversation minutes before. And I see that obsession with unleashing spigots of words by cell phone reflected in many essays that I grade. Hemingway once claimed that having to file stories to a newspaper by telegram/cable forced him to learn to write with economy and to get to the point. Too often my students have difficulty expressing a point – and especially a focused thesis statement. And I believe much of that failure can be attributed to being used to daily undisciplined cell phone use – they become used to saying a lot without saying much that matters. Or, saying a lot before finally meandering to a lucid point. So it is in their essays.

Yes, cell phone use erodes the ability of many students to write well because they have not grown up in a society in which the state of technology restricts them enough to motivate many of them to be focused thinkers and writers. I now thank my lucky stars that I grew up without cell phones – and no computers – until I reached college. Back then I read books. Yes, books! I learned to write well by example and by the technological restrictions of the day. Getting some of my students now to read seems to be akin to asking them to be water boarded.

But at least George Bush and Dick Cheney would be okay with it!

And yes, I do have a cell phone – *traitor!*

But, often I go days without using it. Sometimes I have to look for it if I forget to hook it to a charger. My mom lives in another state and that's how I stay in touch with her. Sometimes I get a call from a colleague or need to call one of them. My cell phone came in very handy once in upstate New York when I had car trouble on a highway and I was able to get Triple A to rescue me.

But, I don't make a call just to hear my voice rattle. Sadly, many people do.

And unfortunately, I can't suggest that my students toss their cell phones in the nearest lake or drainage ditch, though, at the very least, if they disciplined themselves to turn off their phones for days at a time and used them only when they needed them, they might suddenly realize that words are most effective when doled out in sharply focused spurts rather than in perpetual regurgitation.

Teachers can't tell students how to live their lives, but we can factor into our teaching that we must find ways to counter how the grand and elegant English language is being eroded by technology. Many people are willing slaves to technology and like any good addict will live happily in denial – like Charlie Sheen. In online teaching, that means insisting on proper English and spelling in class discussions and e-mail. As a result of the new e-mail etiquette allowing for silly abbreviations and something known as 'lol', those things, too, are popping up in essays. They must be banished.

Hold the line on expecting students to use proper English instead of allowing them to reduce it to unintelligible gibberish and abbreviations, and the language is preserved for another generation, and many students will become, despite their best efforts not to, focused, effective communicators.

I guess I should simply remember two things: I can only fix myself. And two, the dissipation obsession produced by cell phone use means English teachers will always have work – and plenty to fix when it comes to student writing. My job, simply and endlessly, is to help students tame those word geysers into tightly-focused streams of meaning and relevance.

It's a living, as Daffy Duck would say.

Guns, Guns, Guns!
(How GOPism Tries to Take Us Back to the Old West and Make Shoot-Outs a Fun Hobby)

"Happiness is a warm gun."
– *Rocky Raccoon* by The Beatles

I didn't have to think long on what to write this chapter about: the horrible school shootings in Connecticut were just two days ago. If that weren't sad and tragic enough, I am also saddened to realize I am not surprised or overwhelmed by the news. After all, someone shot up Oregon just the other day. And someone recently shot up Denver, too. And Tucson. And my hometown of Jonesboro, Arkansas, a few years back. Just today, I read that someone fired fifty shots at a mall, and a high school kid was arrested for plotting to trick classmates into the school gym, chain the doors, and use bombs and guns to mow them down. In my day, we used to merely skip school or soap windows.

Now students wage trench warfare in their classrooms. Want to learn about Custer's Last Stand? Some deranged wacko who can easily buy a machine gun will re-create it for you.

Wow! Thank you, National Rifle Association.

Thank you, GOPism.

Conservatives never met an assault weapon and good old-fashioned massacre they didn't like.

Custer could only fantasize about having the firepower these school shooters have today as his command was cut to ribbons at Little Big Horn, most of his troopers using single-shot carbines and some of the Indians hefting repeaters.

It's long past time to lay the blame for this senseless violence at the door of the NRA and its puppets in Congress.

And please don't give me the standard GOP claim that guns save lives.

Don't tell me that if teachers and students carried guns this wouldn't happen.

That has never been proven to be true.

Ask Gabby Giffords.

And as a teacher, I don't want armed students when I hand out grades.

Or an armed teacher losing it when a student doesn't understand a comma splice.

Think of the fun we could have, though, if we were all drunk and armed at a bar and someone started an argument or fight.

Shoot, shoot, shoot!

Kill, kill, kill!

The NRA and their GOP surrogates salivate at the thought.

After all, if you still live in the 1800s ideologically, you are just fine with settling disputes with guns. You know, like Jesse James, Billy the Kid, and the Dalton Gang. John Dillinger and Bonnie and Clyde, too. And all those civilians dropping like flies in the crossfires? Just part of the deal. Collateral damage? No biggie – they should have had guns, too!

And remember, if everyone had guns, there'd be no gun violence, right? I mean, that's how it worked in the Old West, right? You walked into a saloon in Dodge City and everyone had a gun and sometimes two or three, plus rifles and shotguns, but no one ever got shot, right?

Maybe ask Wyatt Earp about that if we could.

In those days, sometimes the sheriff waited outside until everyone was out of ammo and the bodies had piled up before risking his own neck.

In the aftermath of Connecticut there will be lots of newspaper columns demanding sensible gun control. The president hinted at it in his remarks right after the shooting. A few television commentators will make impassioned pleas to stop the violence – though, not over at Fox News Fair and Deranged, which will use fake stats and tell lies and perpetuate the myth that guns save lives. Gee, if only those five-year old kids had been packing AK-47s!

Sean Hannity and Drug Addict Rush Limbaugh will call the president a socialist and Kenyan who doesn't understand America for wanting to keep five-year-old children safe from air strikes and helicopter gunships commandeered by teen whackos.

Maybe Sarah Palin will gleefully and maniacally shoot a moose from a helicopter with a bazooka and remind us she can see Russia from her house.

It's not just time for real gun control, folks.

It's well past time for *that*.

It's time to end the NRA. It's a terrorist organization, folks, and it's time to view it that way and starve it from donations any way we can. Vote against any member of Congress who does the bidding of this terrorist organization.

Free Congress from the NRA madness and maybe enough of them will come to their sense and help make laws that truly keep assault weapons out of the hands of whacko.

But I don't expect that will happen as long as we have GOPism.

Instead, the outrage over Connecticut will fade soon and people will forget.

Until the next school gets shot to pieces.

Reality
(You Know, That Concept
Conservatives Avoid at All Costs)

"Well, I've wrestled with reality for 35 years, doctor,
and I'm happy to state I finally won out over it."
    −Elwood P. Dowd, from *Harvey*

But this chapter isn't really about conservatives, though I
bet it gets your attention and I absolutely could go on
forever about the fundamentalist fanatics who claim to
love America (they're lying, folks), but do whatever they
can to strip away democracy.

Instead I want to examine reality from a more
philosophical standpoint and as something impossible to
understand. At least I think it's impossible − Stephen
Hawking, Albert Einstein, Yoda, and Obi-Wan Kenobi
notwithstanding.

Here's how I got going on this: for some reason I
can't explain, a song came into my head the other day.
That's not unusual, though mostly when that happens the
song is something good and ass-kicking − *Gimme
Shelter* by the Stones, *A Day in the Life* by The Beatles,
Taking Care of Business by Bachmann-Turner
Overdrive, *Lola* by the Kinks, *Purple Haze* by Jimi
Hendrix.

All those songs and many more just as great are in
my head and always welcome. They keep the mind

volume up near capacity so that there's no room for me to ever start hearing voices, for example, and feel the need to run for Congress.

But it wasn't one of those songs. It was *Under the Apple Tree*, which is sung by Robert Mitchum in the film *Heaven Knows, Mr. Allison*, a 1957 film directed by John Huston and also starring Deborah Kerr as a nun stranded on a Pacific island during World War II with marine Mitchum and a small garrison of Japanese soldiers. I always figured Mitchum would have much preferred being stranded with, say, Gina Lollobrigida in a bikini instead of Deborah Kerr sweating under all those nun clothes, but that's what he got.

Maybe Gina wasn't available.

And Deborah Kerr got an Academy Award nomination.

Now, I've seen this film at least twice and both times many years ago. It's actually not bad at all. But why that song came into my head now is a mystery, and reality – it's an odd thing that is sort of impossible to figure out.

For example, *Heaven Knows, Mr. Allison* is set in 1944. But remember, it was filmed in 1957. And it was not filmed on any of the Pacific islands where the war with Japan took place. Instead, it was filmed on Tobago and Trinidad, which are in the Caribbean, though it's true that German U-Boats could have ventured near those islands in World War II – but remember, it's 1957 and not 1944 when Mitchum pretends to be a marine and Kerr pretends to be a nun.

And my research reveals that many of the Japanese soldiers in the film were actually portrayed by Chinese who worked on the two islands.

Factor in that when any scene of the film wasn't actually being filmed, Mitchum and Kerr were not their characters and – and neither of them was ever a marine or a nun – and maybe off camera they were eating or sleeping or joking with Huston or reading letters or cavorting with any family that may have been around.

Where's the reality in any of this?

Don't get me wrong – it's a film worth watching. There's a steamy scene where Mitchum and nun Kerr smooch and I suppose that the notion of a marine and a nun lip-locking on an island with some pesky Japanese soldiers lurking about is sort of an Adam and Eve situation. Kind of a humid Garden of Eden.

I guess what I'm saying is that it's all pretty much an illusion. That's certainly what films do – create illusions and thus reality becomes quite the fluid concept.

Sometimes, though, films, in their intent to portray fictional scenes from long ago, inadvertently reveal another way to think of reality. For example, I saw part of a film years ago, just a scene, actually, and I don't remember the actors or even the specific conditions of the scene, but it was a scene in an office building in Chicago. The camera was filming a conversation between characters in an office. The reason I remember this at all is that I was aware that the film was very old. Filmed in the 1930s, I believe. And the reason I can't quite forget this scene is because the camera was positioned so that in addition to seeing the characters involved, there was a clear view of downtown Chicago out a window and off in the distance. I believe I recall seeing the Chicago River. And cars going along a road – Michigan Avenue? Very old and rather primitive cars by today's standards. And you could see tiny people, too – real people from 1930s Chicago. Everything the viewer sees out that window, the people so far away they are small walking figures, are not really fictional fragments of the film. That's really Chicago around 1930.

But I first saw that scene probably ten years ago and so *that* Chicago, the one we can see out the window of the office, no longer exists. Many or even all of the people walking along the street far off from that office window are likely dead. The cars – gone. Not even rusting hulks somewhere, but gone. Metal and plastic and rubber scattered to the winds. Sure, some of the buildings will still be there, but many have changed over time – some even torn down. Any trees that were in that film scene have grown – or were cut down. Businesses visible out that window may have closed or been replaced by different ones over the decades. Time marching on and evolving.

Unlike *Heaven Knows, Mr. Allison*, which attempts to be about 1944 but was shot in 1957 in the Caribbean instead of the Pacific, the film shot in Chicago around 1930 inadvertently allows readers to see beyond the parameters of the film by looking out a window and witnessing the real Chicago of that time. The action taking place outside that window is not scripted or choreographed. It's reality.

But a reality that no longer exists. You are actually seeing it, live at the time it was filmed, but dead at the time you are watching it. Weird, eh? That's what's fun about films shot a long time ago – you become aware that whatever the story, you are nonetheless seeing some place as it really was. In the case of *Heaven Knows, Mr. Allison*, Trinidad and Tobago as they really were in 1957.

Reality.

Except if you watch the film in 2012, that 1957 reality no longer exists.

And Mitchum and Kerr are dead. So is John Huston. Maybe even all the people who portrayed the Japanese soldiers.

If you watch *Heaven Knows, Mr. Allison* tomorrow, you will be seeing Mitchum and Kerr alive and breathing and crying and laughing and loving, and yet you will also be seeing dead people.

So, what's real?

The Tea Party
(Crazy is Crazy No Matter What You Call It)

What is it about democracy that spawns so much affection for tyranny? When I think of the Tea Party faction in Congress, I automatically remember reading about Hermann Goering and his Nazi chums in the German Reichstag. And I'm sure the Tea Party, too, would like to burn down a Reichstag – in this case, Congress.

Yes, folks – I'm comparing the Tea Party to Nazis.

No, folks – I won't apologize or even feel bad about it.

A rose is a rose is a rose, Gertrude Stein wrote.

Nuts is nuts is nuts, when it comes to the Tea Party.

Like Goering and his BFF – Hitler – Tea Party folks are bullies.

And seriously delusional.

And they stand in the way of democracy.

Like Nazis, they are self-righteous destroyers.

They hate democracy because in a democracy the people they hate – minorities, the poor, women, anyone not white and male – have voices.

They claim Obama stole the election because of fraud by Florida election boards.

Despite the fact that the only instances of voter fraud were actually perpetrated by conservatives.

Tea Party whackos claim they want to cut federal spending to reduce the deficit.

That's a lie.

A smokescreen.

Tea Party nut jobs want to end government.

Period.

Not just spending.

They don't want the government to ever help anyone.

Except to keep taxes low on the very rich, of course.

And prosecute wars against anyone who does not agree with the narrowest possible definition of Christianity.

And keep the narrowest and strictest interpretation of the Constitution, which was written so long ago that it could not foresee much of the reality of modern America.

They hate The Affordable Care Act – Obamacare – because it will extend coverage to millions and improves health care in America.

Somehow that's a bad thing to these selfish Tea Party types, who also believe that only property owners should be allowed to vote and state legislatures should pick who goes to Congress.

Elections? We don't need no stinkin' elections.

Elections only result in another term for Muslim Kenyan Socialists like Barack Obama.

Like Goering and his chucklehead Nazi pals, the Tea Party would burn down Congress if it could.

Because God is on their side and wants them to be in charge.

They get e-mail from God all the time.

White wearing their tinfoil hats and playing the radio really loud so that the government and black helicopters can't eavesdrop on them.

The Tea Party is the province of some of the absolutely looniest American politicians – Michelle Bachmann, Sarah Palin, Allen West, Rick Santorum, Jim DeMint.

Of the five above, only Bachmann of Minnesota still held office at the time of this writing.

Thank God.

But what in the world is in the water up in Minnesota?

Fate is a Cat
(No Idea What That Means, But It
Sounds Good)

A few years ago I drove to South Haven, Michigan, to have lunch with a friend aboard The Idler, which is a sort of riverboat converted into a restaurant and moored in South Haven Harbor. I arrived a little early so I could go to the beach and look at Lake Michigan and then swing over to the harbor and walk around.

As I looked out at the harbor and watched boats of many sizes coming and going, I would hear a sound. It would be there and then it wasn't. At first I didn't even know what it might be. It was a faint, inconsistent, squeaking sound, and I figured it could be a plastic boat fender rubbing against a dock. If I cocked my head just right as I walked around the dock area by The Idler, I could hear the sound for a moment, and then it would disappear again.

Across the street from the docks and The Idler are an apartment building and a parking lot in front. Soon my ears picked up the sound again and, like radar, they eventually locked into a location and I crossed the street. On top of a tire of one of the cars parked in the lot was a tiny, orange kitten. It opened its mouth when it saw me, and there was that sound again.

I plucked the kitten from the tire and it seemed awfully glad to see me. It whined and was hungry and thirsty. I got a small box from a nearby store and put the kitten in it and then met my friend for lunch. We ate fish – whitefish from Lake Michigan, I believe it was – with the kitten in the box on my lap. It ate whitefish greedily and I gave it water in a cup.

I drove home to Kalamazoo – about thirty-three miles or so – while trying to hold that kitten and shifting gears in my 1974 Datsun 260 Z, which has manual steering and is a challenge to drive even with two hands. I fought the steering wheel and gear shifter while the kitten fought me to escape. Maybe it was disappointed with the whitefish, but I thought it was quite good. It was a long trip home and I stopped first at the vet that took care of my other cat, EH – much more on EH later. The vet pronounced the kitten to be six weeks old and in good health, but needing the usual medications to clean it up and so I happily took her home.

She became Suzie Lucifer.

As a kitten she was the devil and always up to something.

She was also the result of fate, I guess.

When I first heard her crying near the harbour, I might have simply ignored the sound. But something in me would not let it go. I have rescued cats before – EH was homeless when I found him, for example. Something brought my path across Suzie Lucifer's, just as it had moved me into EH's path one day when I was in graduate school in Kalamazoo. That day I was in a restaurant, looked out a window, saw EH trying to cross a very busy street, and I ran out and scooped him up.

Suzie Lucifer is a big orange cat now, as was EH – he died in 2012. His age was unknown, but when I found him he was perhaps a year old or so and he was with me for nearly eighteen years. Losing him was agony. I had lost a friend who had lived with me in New York,

Wisconsin, Michigan, Texas, and Illinois. He was a loving cat and liked every person he ever met, though he was not at all fond of cats or raccoons and he beat up every cat that made the mistake of straying into his yard, and one night, I pulled him off a raccoon on the back deck. Mind you, he never lost a battle, even without his front claws, which was how he was when I found him. He had more fight in him than any cat I've known and yet he was also calm, gentle, and happy.

Really, until the last months of his life, EH never knew illness or even a bad day. And during his last days he battled and fought to live until there was nothing left. At his peak he weighed more than fifteen pounds and died weighing five pounds. A shell of his former lion self, but right up to the end, the light still shined brightly from his eyes before they closed for good.

This past summer I heard that sound again, the one that led me to Suzie Lucifer in South Haven. I heard it when I walked by an open window of my house and figured it was nothing. I went outside and heard it again. When I looked in the window of my house, Suzie Lucifer was sitting there talking back to me, and I figured that was what I had been hearing.

But something made me go outside again and I heard the sound, and this time Suzie Lucifer was not in the window. Soon my radar ears located the sound in some bushes near my driveway and there was a tiny kitten, mostly white with gray patches. This one was not as easy to capture as Suzie Lucifer had been. It showed surprising energy and speed, and I chased it down several houses from mine.

Like Suzie Lucifer had been, this one, too, was about six-weeks old. Fate had maneuvered another one to me, this time practically to my doorstep. I guess fate had decided it could not take a chance and it was imperative that this one be delivered to me.

She became Yoda Lucifer.

Another devil – and now eight months old and gorgeous, but as a kitten her face really did remind me of Yoda's face.

My house is now full of Suzie Lucifer and Yoda Lucifer and their constant good-natured wrestling.

They have become The Lucifer Sisters.

Loving Devils.

Fate sent them to me.

Thank you, fate.

I don't understand you, but I'm glad you exist.

Moonpie and EH
(The Odd Couple)

EH and Moonpie deserve their own chapter. EH has been gone for such a short time that I still expect to see the huge lion round a corner looking for trouble. Moonpie died well more than a year ago, before the Lucifer Sisters arrived. Moonpie died from some sort of sudden heart failure – a blood clot, perhaps. That's what the vet at the emergency clinic speculated. Without an autopsy, we'll never know. But there was no real reason to do an autopsy. Dead is dead. I was with her when she took her last breath. She was seventeen. A good, long life. Now her ashes are on the fireplace mantle along with EH's. Come the spring I will mix them together in the backyard. They both loved that backyard.

It's funny to recall that during all those many years Moonpie and EH lived together, they rarely paid attention to each other. Even when they napped together on the same bed, it was as though they were actually in separate bedrooms. Moonpie never liked another cat that I can recall. She was a tough little lady – a poet I went to graduate school with dubbed her "The Wicked Queen." She was that. But with me, she was affectionate. While EH was massive and orange, Moonpie was petite, short-legged, and had the look of a cougar. EH would freak out and vomit within minutes of starting any car trip.

Moonpie could be put in a carrier and sit stoically all the way to Alaska if that's how far we were going.

And I made some long trips with them – to Texas, to Wisconsin, and one summer I took Moonpie on the airplane with me when I spent several months north of Los Angeles. EH was too big to fly and I parked him at my mother's house for that summer, and I knew he was in good hands because she was very fond of the big boy. When she used to drive up to Kalamazoo to visit me, I would take EH outside when she pulled up and she would get out and call his name and he would dash over to greet her.

I once drove from Champaign, Illinois, to Canandaigua, New York, with EH and Moonpie, to take a teaching job. Moonpie made the trip without a sound and EH went out of his mind, even with mild sedation provided by the vet. He became essentially Linda Blair in *The Exorcist.* I think Moonpie rather enjoyed watching it. Outside Columbus, Ohio, while at a standstill on the interstate due to backed-up traffic, EH stepped on the window control for the passenger door and I grabbed him by the tail just before he jumped out the window. I think Moonpie was disappointed I rescued him.

Unlike EH, Suzie Lucifer, and Yoda Lucifer, Moonpie wasn't homeless. I wanted a kitten and went to the vet in Champaign to get one. There were a few in a cage and one pushed her way to the front, reached through the bars, and touched her paw to my finger. I knew she was the one. I called her The Moonster, or Moon, or Moonie. She liked being alone, but by the time I came home every day, she was glad to see me before going off on her own again.

Before EH arrived, when it was just Moonpie and I in a second floor apartment in an old Victorian during graduate school, we would play on the hardwood floors. Moonpie would charge me and veer away at the last second and then come back again at me. There were stairs leading from the apartment down to what was the entrance to the apartment, and I would toss rolled up pieces of paper one at a time down the stairs and she would chase them. After a while she would wait at the bottom of the steps for the paper wads to bounce and she would leap to catch them.

The heat for the Victorian was regulated, and in the winter it was always warm enough that some nights I would actually raise a window to bleed off a little heat, and Moonpie would sit in that window for hours sniffing the cold air. I would sometimes awaken and see her still in the window and she would look over at me as if to say, "Still here. Still watching over the house. Don't worry."

She had the reputation of The Wicked Queen, but she was My Little Princess.

My favorite EH story dates back to when I taught at a college in Jacksonville, Illinois, which really is the end of the earth and even having a college there doesn't improve it much. I rented a nice duplex in a neighborhood of good houses, and in nice weather, EH would walk with me around the neighborhood. He was always good about that and would rarely sprint off to see something. He enjoyed just sauntering along beside me, and if he did sometimes stray, I could call his name and he would come back.

One day we walked by the house where another cat lived – the neighborhood bully cat. A cat that sometimes came over to where we lived, and if I had EH outside, this other cat would arrogantly come into the yard and challenge EH's turf. EH was very protective of turf. But this cat was one of the few I ever saw that wasn't afraid of EH and EH could not intimidate him and reluctantly, for probably the only time in his life, EH accepted the presence of an interloper.

But on the day we walked by the other cat's house, both EH and I saw that the garage door was up and we could see the cat asleep in its kitty bed. EH snuck up to the garage and slipped over to the bed and swung a mighty paw right across the cat's head and then ran back to me and stood between my legs. That cat looked awfully surprised and didn't quite know what to do. It finally just sat down near the entrance to the garage and stared back at us.

After that day, EH's nemesis rarely showed up, and when it did, it stayed on the sidewalk and away from our yard.

EH had been victorious yet again.

Daniel Curley
(The Man at the Top of the Stairs)

I'm not sure how famous Daniel Curley was/is and so I place him here in this section rather than the one on Fame. In no way should that seem to diminish my affection for him. Or his importance to me as a writer. Other writers know who Dan was. The late Roger Ebert knew who he was, though plenty of younger folks may not know who Ebert was. Ebert, too, had been one of Dan's students. One of my students plagiarized an Ebert movie review and didn't know who he was. Sadly, Dan was killed by a car in 1988 while crossing a street in Tallahassee, Florida.

I first met Dan around 1980 or so. He was a good short story writer – a winner of the Flannery O'Connor Award – and an English professor at Illinois. The first fiction class I took was with Dan, who also co-authored a book on walking around England with Ebert. Dan was editor of a venerable literary journal, Ascent, and he published Flannery O'Connor, William Gass, Bobbie Ann Mason, and many others.

He even considered one of my first stories because he believed in my potential.

I was introduced to Dan by Joan Klein, another English professor at Illinois. I was in her short story and Shakespeare classes, and she was really the first professor to take an interest in my writing. She was always very kind to me and listened to me patiently before and after class. Even after I graduated, if I was in Champaign, I could show up unannounced at her office and she would invite me in and make time for me.

Dan shared an office with Joan in a rather dingy room at the top of stairs from the third floor of the English Building. As far as offices went, it seemed a bit like a Siberia. Just past their office was Room 313. That was the classroom where my class with Dan was held. It had a blackboard and very old and faded – splintered, in some cases – wooden tables and chairs. No seat in the room was comfortable and there were no pictures on the walls as I recall it.

As classrooms go, it was a Siberia, too.

But before I touch on the first day of class, let me cast back to the day I first met Dan in his small office. Joan made the introductions and I said, "Hey, Dan – how's it going?"

He didn't even hesitate – a hand shot up and a finger wagged and he made it clear it was Prof. Curley and not Dan. He offered me a seat and dutifully intimidated I sat, and can't now recall a single word, though my sense of it is that he was much nicer to me after he had established I was the snotty kid and he was the sage writer who had seen a thing or two. I was then around thirty, but still snotty as far as Dan was concerned.

The first day of class Dan wrote 'Sit at yr. machine' on the blackboard. It's still among the simplest but best writing advice I have encountered because I learned that to write novels I had to commit to writing every day.

Dan had a reputation in those days as a bit of an academic curmudgeon. He could be blunt, direct, and sharp-tongued. One day in class he began to read another student's story and after a few lines Dan said, "Well, that's enough of that and let's put it where it belongs."

125

He promptly dropped the story in the trash can next to his desk.

I recall thinking how glad I was it wasn't my story.

And yet if you got the chance to know Dan, he could be very nice and fun.

It was getting past his front gate that was difficult.

From him I began to understand why writers often need to protect their time.

But I also recall that I used to pester him with questions about writing before and after class and one day I apologized for it, saying I didn't mean to take up so much of his time. He said, "No one else is asking and so you may have their time, too."

After I graduated from Illinois, I moved to Arizona to be a newspaper reporter and Dan and I passed a few letters. Around 1984 or 1985 I wrote to him that I'd be visiting Champaign and he wrote back to come by for a visit. His wife let me into their house and announced she would go run some errands. "To give you boys some room."

"Let's see what there is to drink," Dan said with a smile and a wink. We found a bottle of Southern Comfort in a kitchen cabinet and we drank a good amount of it straight – neat, as they say.

Our afternoon lasted a few hours. Dan told me I had excellent potential to write fiction when I was ready to really get serious about it. I was not yet ready. That would come almost ten years later. But that afternoon Dan and I talked about writing in great detail and he was happy to answer my questions and he encouraged me to get serious about writing. He told me about famous writers he had met and I told him I had just met Erskine Caldwell in Arizona, which surprised him.

"I thought he was dead," Dan said, shaking his head.

"Almost," I said.

I remember that Dan told me about his friendship with Carson McCullers. I know that he told me a funny story about her and swimming, but I don't recall enough of the details.

Then Dan said a writer was coming to campus to read and he had been asked to introduce him.

"Do you know much about this Ray Carver?" Dan said.

Dan didn't really know who Raymond Carver was.

But, back then Carver was just making his bones and I told Dan that Carver was an exciting new writer, and with a laugh he said he'd be sure to find out just who he was before standing up to introduce the man.

When Dan was killed in 1988, I had just moved back to Champaign and my mom told me the sad news. Dan and his wife were crossing a street in Tallahassee and a driver hit them both, killing Dan instantly and badly injuring her.

He was a good man. A good writer. Much nicer than many people realized. There were more books in him, I'm sure, and literature was deprived of them. I lost a friend and the first real writer who told me I was good enough to be a real writer, too.

To some degree it was his confidence in me as a writer that enabled me to become confident in myself. Every time I finish writing a novel, I wish I could show it to him.

I know he would be proud of me.

And maybe he'd tell me he told me so.

The Arts

The Myth of Rap and the Glory of Jimi Hendrix
(We Miss You, Man)

Well, I know this will bring criticism, but it's my book and my beliefs, folks, and so here goes: Rap "music", or hip-hop "music", or whatever the current designation for it is, is not music at all.

Now, I know that some readers might try and label me as somehow intolerant because I don't think rap is music, and so by extension I must be criticizing or even demeaning African-Americans. Not true. And race is pretty much irrelevant to the discussion. If rap had been invented by snotty and rich white teens in Grosse Pointe, Michigan, I still wouldn't consider it music or even to be very musical. And by the way, I'm also not a fan of country music, though country music is at least indeed musical. Does that mean I'm somehow against folks in silly cowboy hats who tout the military but wouldn't actually serve their country? I also don't care for opera – but I concede it's musical. And I have nothing against beefy men and women with voices that could strip paint off a wall.

So, what is rap?

Frankly, it's loud talking.

It's loud talking by snarling men and women.

On stages with a lot of tedious hand signals and posturing that I don't quite fathom.

If you need a lot of style, you don't have much substance.

And given how warm it might be inside some of those arenas, why wear hooded sweatshirts and winter coats with the hoods pulled up?

More silly and tedious posturing.

And to what end?

But, a minor issue, I concede.

Mostly I worry they might pass out from the heat.

Or from the venom in their lyrics.

Now, I do understand and believe that rap is a form of artistic expression.

That sometimes it reflects observations on culture, society, and community conditions.

And sometimes – too often – it's merely snarly, misogynist, violent, and crude.

I'm willing to concede that rap is a performance of sorts.

And here's another way I look at rap: it's a cheap way to attain fame and wealth. I believe Keith Richards has called it "music" for people who are tone deaf. Something like that. I always defer to Keef on these matters.

Rap is a means to be rich and famous without apparent musical talent.

It's a time on stage for people who can't sing.

Rap doesn't require singing.

Or actual ability to play an instrument.

Doing whatever rap folks do with vinyl albums – that grating, annoying scratching noise it produces – doesn't count as musical.

And just about anyone can do rap (well, probably not most Republicans).

But not everyone can be Jimi Hendrix. Or Keith Richards.

Hendrix has been dead around forty-six years and yet still rates as the top guitarist of all time, even though his career was so brief.

There are some other great guitarists, but not so many – Keith Richards is my favorite – and they don't top Hendrix.

A record company could throw money at someone average and that average person would still not become Jimi Hendrix or Keith Richards.

But a rap label, if it really wanted to, could throw money and time at many people and make them into a rap "star."

Yes, they could.

Because it's mostly just talking a certain way.

Dressing a certain way.

Acting a certain way.

Style over substance.

And it's not art.

Sorry to feel that way, folks.

But I won't pretend.

I know some of you will be offended.

But if just about anyone can do something, it's not really art.

Jimi Hendrix is art.

Keith Richards is art.

Of course, some conservative parents in the 1960s and beyond moaned that rock music was awful, too.

And just noise.

Listen to The Who and the Rolling Stones and Led Zeppelin – and especially the album *Full House* by the J. Geils Band.

That's a loud album.

But it's not just loud.

It's music.

It really is.

Rap – not so much.

Ghosts as a Growth Industry
(But at Least They Seem More Real
Than the Kardashians)

Ghosts. What a concept. People without bodies. Unless they're apparitions, of course, and then they *sort* of have bodies – wispy, gaseous, foggy, bodies that can pass through doors and walls. How cool! I wish I could do that sometimes. That's high on the fantasy list, just below playing safety for the Chicago Bears, jamming with Keith Richards and the Stones, and having Scotty beam me aboard the Starship Enterprise. Sex with Renee Russo – that's up there, too. I hope you're reading this, Renee.

But back to ghosts. I'm writing this because I just saw an ad on TV for *Ghost Hunters*, a popular and surprisingly entertaining reality show, and apparently ghost hunting is quite the growth industry. I have actually watched perhaps as many as twenty or more episodes over several of its eight seasons. At the time of this chapter, I believe it's entering a ninth season (did even *Seinfeld* last that long?).

Despite my affection for the show, I no longer believe in ghosts.

Although I did when I first started watching *Ghost Hunters*.

Now I don't – thanks, *Ghost Hunters*!

You made a believer out of me.

Just not the way you'd like.

But I still watch the show sometimes because I like its main stars – Grant, Jason, Steve, and Tango, even though I'm not quite sure why because they believe in ghosts and I lost that belief thanks to their hard work and personal sacrifices to their families. I lost my belief despite the hard work of the show, which purports to scientifically debunk what can be explained, and what is truly, in their eyes, paranormal.

But, at least the show is more fun than those dreadfully narcissistic Kardashians.

Hell, ghosts are more likeable than the Kardashians.

And ghosts are far better role models, too.

And ghosts have more substance than any Kardashian you choose to pick, which is saying quite a bit since ghosts really have no substance at all.

Now, don't get me wrong – it's not that I can't think outside the box, which is one of the worst and now most tedious sayings I ever heard. For example, I still believe in the JFK conspiracy, no matter what recent investigations have concluded. And I've already mentioned my views on the moon landing in 1969.

And I still believe that George W. Bush is the love child of aliens and some escaped mental patient.

And disco may have been a CIA plot to rot our brains.

And the Bee Gees? Men with their balls caught in vices.

But ghosts? Call me skeptical.

Yes, I have even had one experience that maybe was paranormal. *Maybe. Perhaps.* One night at a bed and breakfast in St. Cloud, Minnesota, on a hot evening, the fan positioned toward me in bed suddenly shifted 180 degrees in another direction. I reset it and a few hours later – bam! It moved again. The owners of the place said a man died there many years before and they believe it's now haunted.

Or maybe the fan just spins a little out of control sometimes.

And if it was a ghost – was that the best it had that night?

It must be boring to be a ghost if you pass the time by moving fans around.

Any ghost worth a damn would instead sing *The Macarena* while giving a wedgie to someone sleeping.

But back to *Ghost Hunters*, which I hope stays on TV because I do like it and I worry that Grant, Jason, Steve, and Tango would become depressed and bored if they had to go back to working for Roto-Rooter or any other nine-to-five existence. Grant recently left the show and for reasons that in his initial announcement seemed as murky as an apparition. Maybe he's trying to save his marriage and family, which probably suffers mightily when your job means spending a lot of nights at somebody's else's house.

And here's another problem with *Ghost Hunters* or any other reality show that claims to hang out with ghosts: Where's the real proof? Every time they show up at some "haunted" place, they get all gooey and excited and set up their cameras because someone told them there are floating apparitions and severed heads (okay, I made that one up) dancing along the chandeliers.

Sounds promising, I admit – though, Eddie Murphy once said, "If the chandelier starts talking, my little back ass is out of there!"

Eddie should know – his career has become ghostly. Like an apparition – we see right through it.

But back to the apparitions on *Ghost Hunters*, which we never see.

I never have, anyway.

And why can't the *Ghost Hunters* team do an investigation until the lights are turned off at the haunted location?

Can't ghosts see in the dark?

When the lights are on, do ghosts sort of loiter off camera smoking cigarettes and getting annoyed that no one has switched off the lights and cued them to the scene yet?

"Yo, apparition – you're up, dude! And for God's sake – try to be scary, you Casper candyass!"

And since ghosts don't have actual bodies – no eyes – then what difference does it make whether the room is dark or lit? Or whether it's day or night? Why do all of these investigations start when the sun is down? Don't ghosts have anything to do during the day?

Do they hang with the vampires?

Are they sleeping?

If you don't have a body, do you really need to sleep?

Are ghosts off somewhere during the day watching the Kardashians?

Without eyes, would they be able to see the Kardashians?

What a blessing if they can't.

Here's another thing: every now and then the *Ghost Hunters* team catches sounds on their recorders. And I'll admit there have been times when I thought those sounds did actually seem like voices.

But if ghosts lack bodies – and thus no vocal chords – how can they speak?

So, call me skeptical, but highly entertained by the show.

If *Ghost Hunters* really wants to show me something scary and other-worldly, they should invite me down into the basement of some haunted house and shine a light on the Kardashians.

The Death of Rock and Roll
(Long Live Rock!)

I'm not exactly sure when rock and roll died. But it did. Long live rock!

But if you need proof, just remember that nowadays most kids grow up wanting to talk on a stage and make spitting sounds instead of wanting to learn how to sing or play guitar. After all, it sure cuts down on the time involved to become famous and have a reality TV show about your mansion if you don't actually have to be able to create music.

Sometimes I think rock and roll died in the early 1980s, but I suppose it could have been much earlier. Some folks might say it died as early as 1969-70 because The Beatles had left the stage for good and Jimi Hendrix, Janis Joplin, and Jim Morrison had all died of their excesses.

I wonder if rock actually lasted until the 80s because the Rolling Stones were then still going strong, even though they were no longer producing albums as great as *Let It Bleed*, or *Beggar's Banquet*, or *Exile on Main Street*, or *Sticky Fingers* – or even the lesser but underrated *Goat's Head Soup*.

The first album I ever bought was the Stones' fifth – *December's Children* – in 1965. When you get to *Route 66* and *Get off My Cloud* on *December's Children*, you hear the Stones taking a step toward becoming the world's greatest rock and roll band.

Even in 2012, the amazing 50th anniversary of the band, the Stones made many other bands seem puny and unoriginal.

And who is really playing rock anymore? Paul McCartney is still out there playing his greatest hits and some of The Beatles'. I loved The Beatles and love McCartney, but he's a barrel of hair color removed from the Fab Four. And John Lennon and George Harrison are long gone. Ringo Starr is a curiosity.

What replaced rock? Nothing. Sadly, we have for some time been inundated with rap, which I wrote about in a previous chapter. I can barely come up with the names of any bands today playing rock. Foo Fighters? They come to mind mostly because by chance I watched a documentary on them and realized I like Dave Grohl. But when he recently performed with Paul McCartney and the other Nirvana survivors, I thought the song was half-baked noise.

And don't get me started on Nirvana, which doesn't even really have a body of work. When Curt Cobain died it was sad, but apparently rather inevitable, and when folks started turning him into John Lennon, I was horrified. Lennon had a body of work. Cobain had three albums and a shotgun. Cobain's death did not remind me of Jimi Hendrix, or Keith Moon, or Jim Morrison, or Brian Jones, or Janis Joplin, or John Lennon, or George Harrison.

And certainly not Elvis.

Beyond whenever it was that rock died, we have had The Void.

Since rock died, we've had hair bands, boy bands, and Milli Vanilli.

But apparently we still have the Stones, and who would have thought, back in 1962 when wispy and fragile Brian Jones started the band, that they would last fifty years.

Hell, who thought Keith Richards would see forty?

I'm glad he did. But now he looks 100.

Cockroaches and Keith Richards, as the old joke goes, will be the only survivors of nuclear war.

Or, as comedian Denis Leary once said, "There are no more drugs to abuse – Keith Richards took them all!"

But Keith is one of my heroes.

And he seems to have shed addiction to all the drugs except the one he needs the most – playing guitar in a real rock band.

"I know, it's only rock and roll, but I like it!"
-The Rolling Stones

The Death of the Movies
(Not Really, But It's Catchy)

Unlike rock and roll, the film industry isn't dead.

But sometimes I think it's on life support.

Or in a coma.

Or maybe it's just that we must accept that for one really good film every now and then, we must endure a dozen or more that are crap.

Special effects extravaganzas.

Hollywood wakes up from the coma, has a cup of coffee, and then slips back into it.

Part of the problem is that the industry is still, and likely always will be, dominated by rich people very out of touch in their California mansions and New York apartments. Some of those rich and out of touch folks actually once were in touch and not rich. Brad Pitt came from a small town in Missouri. Tom Cruise is from upstate New York.

Don't get me wrong, I'm not accusing Pitt and Cruise of being great actors.

Sometimes they're good in a role and sometimes they're a pretty face in a role.

Sometimes Cruise is perplexing in a role.

He often lacks – true humanity.

I *will* accuse the following actors of being pretty damn good: Daniel Day-Lewis, Cate Blanchett, Colin Firth, Tom Hanks, Meryl Streep.

There are others, to be sure.

But not so many.

And I will accuse Rene Russo of being the answer when I'm asked which actress would I most like to – romance.

But back to movies. When people think of the greatest movies, inevitably we hear names that I disagree with – *Casablanca* and *Citizen Kane*. I could check, but I'm confident that many of the lists of the top 100 movies still have those two at the top.

I shrug when *Casablanca* and *Citizen Kane* are mentioned. They're just two old black and white films that don't seem that much better than many other old black and white movies, like *To Kill a Mockingbird*, which certainly ranks well on movie lists, too.

But for decades rich and out of touch folks in New York and California have perpetuated the CasaKane myths.

Frankly, I'd rather watch The Beatles in *A Hard Day's Night*, another black and white film on the lists.

Really, though – I don't have a thing against black and white films other than the obvious limitations they have.

Ask me to make my list of top movies and at number one I tend toward *Lawrence of Arabia*.

Just a feeling.

The first time I saw it I was very stoned and it was magnificent.

The second time I saw it I wasn't stoned at all and it was still magnificent.

Casablanca and *Citizen Kane*? Perhaps in the top twenty-five and toward the bottom half of that.

That's just me. I don't feel obligated to worship the New York and Beverly Hills film intelligentsia. But at least I'm not rich and out of touch, though I could warm up to the rich part.

And by the way, the best film in a given year doesn't always win the Oscar for best picture.

In 1969 *Butch Cassidy and the Sundance Kid* lost to *Midnight Cowboy*.

Ugh! Give me a break – or, as John McEnroe might say, "You cannot be serious!"

My theory is that Butch and the Kid is a great film that allowed its Achilles heel to show and was nipped at the finish line because it kept the scene where "Raindrops Keep Falling on My Head" is the equivalent of someone pissing on the Mona Lisa.

Okay – maybe the Mona Lisa is a bit of a stretch in this analogy, but you get the idea. Everything about Butch and the Kid is going great until that scene, where basically a great film takes a break to offer a commercial for a song that was popular at the time.

Big Mistake.

Fast forward to 1999 and *Saving Private Ryan* loses the Oscar to *Shakespeare in Love.*

Really? A great film that is about ideas and not just war, as Roger Ebert wrote, gets nipped by fluffy Shakespeare Gets a Woody?

One more time, John McEnroe.

"You cannot be serious!"

But maybe my favorite example is when *Titanic* took the 1999 Oscar for best film.

Apparently voters were seduced by the fact that, yes, that film likely does depict the sinking as it really must have looked better than previous films about Titanic.

But for me, that's where the film's greatness ends.

It is, after all, a second-rate re-telling of history featuring a standard and third-rate stereotypical Hollywood romance. But nice effects, of course! And wispy Leo DiCaprio had not yet learned to be an actor and was still relying on being a pretty face.

See Tom Cruise.

See dozens of other pretty faces.

Anyway – look at this best picture process this way: in competitive diving, degree of difficulty is important. As I understand it, a diver can attempt a hard dive or one not so hard, and doing really well with a hard dive can garner more of a score than doing well with a less-ambitious dive.

You can score with the average gal at the dance, or Rene Russo, and Rene earns you more slaps on the back.

Titanic does not seek a very high degree of difficulty.

But one of the other nominees that year, *The Full Monty*, does.

Think about what *The Full Monty* attempts: it's a redemption story – I love redemption stories – that says unemployed and out of shape steel workers in Sheffield, England, will magically become Chippendale-quality male strippers and earn back respect from family and community and self-respect for themselves.

Oh really?

Folks, that degree of difficulty is off the charts.

And yet *Monty* does it. It pulls it off. Literally pulls it off – their clothes!

The film is full of charm and quirks and by the end we have laughed out loud and have come to love Gaz, Dave, Gerald, and their buddies. And so do their families and community.

All that seemed improbable at the beginning.

And far more ambitious than Titanic, which is special effects and lots of money and an expensive promotion campaign. It reflects the Hollywood of rich and out of touch.

I scored *Titanic* as dead last among the nominees, with *Good Will Hunting*, a surprisingly thoughtful film, in the number two spot behind *The Full Monty*.

With *Titanic,* Hollywood had gone back into its coma and expected the rest of us to join it.

Places

Places

Twenty-Four Hours in Paris
(Looking for Hemingway's Footsteps)

I had always wanted to see Paris after reading Hemingway's *A Moveable Feast* in the early 1980s. So around 1991 or so I hopped a plane from Chicago. I remember the plane actually had a little moving plane on a map you could look up at to see where we were at the moment – you know, over Newfoundland, or Labrador, or the middle of the North Atlantic or whatever you must fly over when you spend the equivalent of a work day in an airplane.

I shared a taxi from De Gaulle with a nice young woman from Minneapolis, I think it was – or maybe Milwaukee. Like me, she was making her first visit to Paris. I intended to take the taxi on to my hotel after we dropped her off, but when we got to her hotel, the taxi driver emphatically announced that there was a strike and he could not cross the Seine. So, carrying two bags, I ended up on the Metro. At the counter I pushed a wad of very pretty French money to the clerk and he grinned and took what he wanted, which I am still sure was more than he needed. Ah, to be American in Paris without knowing the language.

But the money sure was pretty.

Naturally, having to take the Metro to get to my hotel on Rue Victor Cousin was just the start of my adventure. A young man with a very large and menacing German Shepherd came into the car I was in, and the dog began to growl at me. I must have given the wrong look in reply because the young man began what I was sure were some choice French insults, and so I did the math quickly in my head: I figured I could take the kid, but not the dog – certainly not both of them – and so I got off at the next stop.

I wasn't sure how to get back on track toward my hotel and so I asked an elderly woman if she spoke English, but she didn't. I spoke the words "Rue Victor Cousin" and she smiled and grabbed my arm and steered me toward a sign and pointed: it was for St. Germaine. I got off at that stop but learned that although I had ended up walking along a very narrow street flanked by beautiful old buildings – still carrying two bags – I was not necessarily on track for the street my hotel was on.

And so I wandered. At first it was not so bad because any direction I looked it was Paris and it was fascinating to see. I walked by a restaurant with sidewalk tables covered with brilliant white tablecloths and when I paused to ask a waiter about Rue Victor Cousin, he pretended that I had actually said, "Table for one."

I took streets at random. The weather was good. It was a sunny day, the temperature moderate, and I knew that if I kept walking it was inevitable that I would wind up somewhere and that I had to eventually find someone who would steer me to Rue Victor Cousin. Finally, I saw a gendarme ahead and I figured my problems were over. The gendarme even spoke English. But he professed no knowledge of Rue Victor Cousin, which at first struck me as plausible and that perhaps he was a cop who really hadn't yet learned all the streets. Of course, I knew that theory was all wrong and the truth was that he likely took pleasure in snubbing an American who didn't have the decency to know French because the very next street I came to was Rue Victor Cousin and my hotel was just a few blocks down it across from the Sorbonne.

The next morning, I left the hotel to see a little bit of Paris. I walked by the Luxembourg Gardens and saw Notre Dame Cathedral. I sat outside a café like a real Parisian – a real American pretending to be a real Parisian – and drank Kronenbourg beer, which is French beer, and I thought that was a good choice, although the waiter was so inattentive and slow that I realized it could take all day to get drunk.

I had taken a book with me called *Hemingway's Paris*. I believe I still have it – up on the fireplace mantle along with my Tom Tresh outfielder's mitt from Little League and the ashes of my cats EH and Moonpie. I drifted around and stopped at several Hemingway landmarks – La Closerie des Lilas among them – but quickly I realized how foolish I was to believe there was such a thing as Hemingway's Paris. I had always loved "A Good Café on the Place St. Michel" from *A Moveable Feast* and had always wanted to sit at a café and see and hear and smell Paris as Hemingway did. But that Paris is long dead. It was obvious everywhere I went. Too many years had come and gone. Looking for Hemingway's Paris was a fool's errand now. And everywhere I went, I also learned that not knowing French and being American in Paris would not be much of a picnic. I even began to tell people I was Canadian.

And then just barely twenty-four hours after I had arrived, I made an impulsive and stunning decision: I went home. I asked the clerk at the hotel to check me out and at first he eyed me incredulously and kept asking me if I really was leaving. After asking me as many as four or five times, thinking surely I was just a joking

American, he believed me, we settled my bill, and he called me a taxi for De Gaulle.

The taxi was a Mercedes and it was driven by a young and smiling Vietnamese man. He helped me stow my bags in the trunk and we were off – like a rocket-propelled grenade. He became Mario Andretti behind the wheel and we roared down narrow streets as I clutched that little hand strap hanging down by my head. Soon, my driver looked over his shoulder at me, which scared the crap out of me considering how fast we were going, and he said, "So you Americans like to party?"

I said, "Well, I like a party as much as anyone, I suppose."

After another minute or two my driver looked back at me again and said, "So, you Americans like to party," and then I knew, of course, that he didn't speak English and that was pretty much how it went as we streaked like a bat out of hell out to De Gaulle and never in my life was I so happy to get out of a car. I tipped him with some of that pretty French money and he pulled away from the curb like he was shot out of a cannon. I was tempted to pray for his safe return to the city. I also vaguely wondered whether he was old enough to have been in the Vietcong.

Inside the airport, I found a little snack bar and I tried to order something. The sweet teenage girl behind the counter spoke excellent English and she was quite friendly, and that reminded me that not everyone in France hates Americans. But I do think a good amount of them delight in messing with Americans. I resisted the temptation to remind them about the Americans who died at Normandy, for example, but didn't because it's not so simple as that and it's not like I was even alive then and knew any of them and so, really, what would have been the point?

I asked the girl behind the counter if they had any real breakfast food – eggs, bacon, sausages, pancakes – because I suddenly felt like breakfast food and all I saw in the little snack bar were pastries and breads and the young girl laughed rather lustily, actually, and informed me with an exaggerated tone that, "No, monsieur – we don't have the big American breakfast." And so even this otherwise nice and pleasant young girl also delighted in messing with Americans.

I took my orange juice and pastries to a table and the pastries were quite good and it felt good to sit and just watch people pass by while I waited for my flight. Soon a squad of men and women from somewhere in the Middle East approached my table. Actually, they all stopped a few yards short of my table and studied me rather coldly as one of them, a man in a very nice suit, came over and in very good English asked whether I would be troubled if they all shared my table. It was a very large table with many chairs and I didn't mind at all. I thought it might be interesting to talk with my new tablemates and maybe even ask them how they got along with the locals.

Instead I discovered that no matter what I asked or how friendly I tried to be, they had no intention of conversing with me. I simply wasn't there as far as they were concerned. They just wanted the table and sitting with an American was the somewhat tolerable price of it. I grabbed my bags and urged them to enjoy the table, but not a one of them said a word or even made eye contact with me.

Maybe they were just having a bad day.

But I was having a good day now that I had survived my taxi ride and was soon to head home via Chicago, which is probably where I should have gone in the first place and saved some money. I got on the plane with a spring in my step, settled into a seat, and barely seconds after we took off, I fell asleep.

I slept long enough for the plane to get far out over the Atlantic – oh, and let me say here, because I forgot to mention earlier, that on the incoming flight I had a spectacular view of Land's End in Britain as we settled into our approach to Paris and it was quite an amazing sight and now, when people ask me where to stay in Paris, I say, "London."

But back to the outgoing flight. We're out over the ocean and my eyes are slowly focusing as I wake up, and when they do focus, I see smoke billowing toward me in the cabin and I think, how odd to survive a taxi ride piloted by a Samurai Vietnamese only to wake up in an airplane on fire. And over an ocean, as I mentioned before. I very nearly slipped my seatbelt and jumped out of my seat except that when I took a second look at the oncoming smoke, I realized it was smoke billowing in the in-flight movie. An Air France attendant asked me if I was okay and impulsively I said just about the only French I knew, which was, "Je suis American."

When we landed at O'Hare, I had time to kill before my short flight down to Champaign, and so I found a bar and drank a very cold Leinenkugel's beer and ate several hot dogs with onions and gobs of mustard and French fries drowned in ketchup and I thought that cold beer from Wisconsin and Chicago hot dogs never tasted so good.

After a while, several burly guys sat at the table next to me and one of them asked me how the beer was. I nodded enthusiastically, raised my mug and said, "Hey, how about those Bears?"

Key West

(More Hemingway Footsteps)

Like Paris, Key West was a place I always wanted to see because of Hemingway. I had read his posthumous novel *Islands in the Stream*, which came out in 1970, and by 1974 I was on a plane first to Miami and then Key West and I arrived quite drunk. But I felt Hemingway would have understood. And would have joined in.

Key West is so small you can easily walk across it, and the taxi ride from the tiny airport to my hotel took about seventeen seconds, I think it was – like that scene in *LA Story* where Steve Martin gets in his car and drives fifty feet to his neighbor's house. I stayed at The Pier House, which was – and hopefully still is – right on the water, and in 1974, anyway, there was a restaurant nearby called the A&B Lobster House and supposedly Errol Flynn liked to eat there. I ate there, too, and my table overlooked docks and a little harbor and I saw a very large tarpon suddenly leap completely out of the water and crash back into it in a frothy spray. Maybe that was Errol Flynn reincarnated.

Or, as Sigmund Freud would say, sometimes a tarpon is just a tarpon.

After I sobered up, I did the standard Hemingway tour – his house, Sloppy Joe's, Captain Tony's. His house was built in 1851 and if I remember correctly, there was a small Picasso painting hanging over his bed that Picasso gave to him because they were old drinking buddies in his Paris days. Nice. The most I ever had above my bed was a poster of Walter Payton or Dick Butkus when they played for the Bears. I guess that little Picasso would be worth more than most people's houses.

Unlike Paris, Hemingway's footprints still seemed to litter Key West in those days. I suppose they still do. The house is a museum and people can get a sense of what his home life must have been like with second wife Pauline. I could imagine Hem drinking at Sloppy Joe's with cronies, or his first meeting with Martha Gellhorn, who would become his third wife. Paris, I think, keeps moving well beyond its famous citizens and visitors, but Key West is still a Hemingway Mecca. His footprints are still all over the place.

My first night in Key West, I was drinking in a joint – not Sloppy Joe's and perhaps the bar at the Pier House – and I got into conversation with several people about fishing. I was sitting at the bar with these old salts and also a sprinkling of rich folks living on their sailboats, and one of them said he was captain of a charter boat. Now in 1974, even a guy like me, just four years out of high school and working at my stepfather's appliance store, could afford a day charter. I don't recall the price, but I think it was only about $200. Nowadays a day's charter can be quite expensive, but I had saved money for quite a while to make the trip and fishing was figured into my budget. The charter captain asked for $100 up front and told me he and his mate would pick me up at sunrise at a dock near The Pier House.

The next morning, I waited on the dock and I admit it crossed my mind that the guy wasn't a charter captain at all and I had merely donated $100 to his night of drinking. But soon an impressive boat with a flying bridge and outriggers and downriggers on the stern came alongside the dock and the captain waved me aboard. I can't recall what he or his mate looked like. Or names. My sense of it is that the mate was a little older than me and the captain was in his forties and both were very tan. I must have looked very much like the pale northerner that I was. Growing up in Illinois, we would get light summer tans, but a Key West tan appeared to burn all the way into the bone. It could make a forty-year-old man look much older.

Once out of harbor and into the Gulf Stream we steered toward Cuba, but of course we would not go quite that far. But it was exciting to think of Castro's Cuba just ahead beyond the horizon, and it made me think, too, of another Hemingway novel, *To Have and Have Not,* which was about folks smuggling between Cuba and Florida and so we were sailing the waters that book also sailed.

The captain steered stoically, eyes on the horizon, and the mate prepped the rods and reels and there was also a large cooler of ice with beer and water, and for lunch there were barbecue sandwiches – pork, I think – slathered in sauce dripping from the bread, and they were quite tasty. After a while, the captain waved me up to join him on the bridge, but that was not as easy as it looked because I had to climb a ladder that tilted rather sideways and as the boat pitched and rolled, the ladder was a moving target and no easy climb up to the bridge, where there was only a narrow metal railing that one put the small of the back into. But the view from up there was terrific and the captain let me steer a few minutes so I could pretend to be an old salt, too. I began to know how Hemingway must have felt and how happy he must have been when he sailed the Gulf Stream in his own boat, *Pilar.*

Ostensibly, we had gone out that day looking for marlin, the magnificent and noble species that so captivated Hemingway. He caught many of them and there are many photos of a beaming Hem posing with the creatures. At one point the captain said he thought he saw a marlin's sail and he even put the boat into a sudden turn to backtrack over the water he believed the marlin might still be in, but I never saw it and the captain finally gave up on it, conceding his eyes may have simply played tricks on him. I wondered how it must have been aboard *Pilar* with Hem at the wheel searching for a marlin's sail.

The lack of marlin didn't spoil the day. We caught yellowtail tuna, Spanish mackerel, and grouper. And I caught two barracuda, which were the highlight of the day. As I recall, the barracuda struck suddenly and hard and made quite the show of leaping out of the sea and dancing on their tails, twisting, gyrating, and trying to dislodge the hook. The mate always slipped on gloves to bring a barracuda on board because of the razor-sharp teeth.

When we stopped for lunch and beer, I felt as if there could be no finer existence than to fish from a boat in the Gulf Stream. I felt I knew very much why it appealed so strongly to Hemingway. I would look off at the water, the horizon, and felt I could almost see the *Pilar* and bearded old Hem, a bit of a pirate happily steering and sipping a drink. Perhaps, more than was possible in just about any other place on earth, on his boat he felt free of the complications of wives and children and life in a society where he was a famous man everyone wanted to meet.

New York
(The Big Old Damn Apple)

In February of 2011, I made my first trip to New York City as an adult. My family had visited there in the early 1960s and back then we went to the Empire State Building and attended the "Garry Moore Show," which delighted my mother, who is a Carol Burnett fan. I can still see an image of the studio, and for some reason, the show's applause sign stands out in my memory. Maybe because of the notion that the show's producers didn't trust an audience to applaud and had to take matters into their own hands, so to speak.

Why do I call New York the big old damn apple? Because I have very mixed feelings about the place. I really much prefer Chicago and have no desire to live in New York City, even though I know many people see it as sort of an Oz that all golden paths should ultimately lead to. I'm very suspicious of places where average people can't afford a home or even rent a respectable apartment – not that Chicago's cheap, mind you.

But I do admit that my second trip to The Big Apple was pleasant. I had flown in from Michigan to meet my agent, Pauline Vilain, for the first time. She died unexpectedly in April 2012. A huge loss. She was my friend as well as my agent.

Pauline flew over from The Netherlands and it was her first trip to America. I suggested to her that seeing

New York as the first look at what America is about is as faulty as thinking that Paris as a first look at France is somehow reliable. I just don't see New York City as the center of any universe. Not my universe, anyway. Of course, when it comes to publishing, which is certainly something I need, New York still clings to a rather Napoleonic notion of itself as the center of things. I don't deny that it's where the big publishers are, but it would be healthy for New York editors to get out of New York more. America between New York and Los Angeles is not just flyover territory.

But I admit that New York is an amazing metropolis. When my flight there arrived, we went into a long holding pattern, which was actually good because we were rather low and circled the city a number of times and it really gave me perspective on how big it is. And many New Yorkers are certainly friendlier than some Parisians. Really, almost everyone I met and interacted with in New York was pleasant. Luck of the draw? Perhaps. I had a Russian taxi driver who welcomed a long conversation, and because he had lived there twenty-five years and knew the city, he gave me a fun and informative tour of the place when he ran me out to LaGuardia for the flight home.

I was in Manhattan three days and stayed at The Salisbury on West 57th Street. A short walk from Central Park and Fifth Avenue. It's an affordable hotel and the people were very friendly, but it doesn't have a restaurant or bar, which actually is not so bad at all given that just a couple doors down the street is Angelo's, a delightful restaurant that claims Madonna and David Letterman as patrons. I looked around, but no Dave or Material Girl. I was disappointed because I could have finagled them into more chapters.

The crown jewel of my New York trip was the Museum of Modern Art. Pauline and I spent an afternoon there and I saw many works of art I had known about most of my life, but had never seen up close. For example, Dali's *Persistence of Memory*, a work I have always loved, is tiny and I always supposed it was large. Monet's *Water Lilies*, which I presumed to be small, is actually immense. That Rousseau painting whose title I always forget – the sleeping peasant watched by a lion – is bigger than I expected. I also saw works by Picasso, Cezanne, Degas, Matisse, and Kandinsky. The vibrancy of Kandinsky's colors surprised me and I was pleasantly overwhelmed when I entered that room. My old web site borrowed Kandinsky colors for its background.

In New York the February weather was surprisingly mild and one could walk around at night. I recall a bar on 57th Street that apparently wants to be an imitation of Paris in the 1800s. It was pleasant enough, but employees seemed to outnumber patrons. Must have been an off night. It was so dark there that if people sat down naked, one might not notice for a while. I much prefer the far less pretentious Billy Goat Tavern in Chicago. It has good lighting and its rich history flows from the many photographs on the walls.

But those Manhattan days were genuinely fun and interesting. Pauline and I took a cab down to Tribeca and then up past Hell's Kitchen, and visited some bookstores to see if they would carry my books. Everyone was nice, polite, and surprised, I suspect, that someone from the Midwest would show up with his books. I couldn't help but feel just a little like Jon Voight's character in *Midnight Cowboy*.

Chicago, Chicago, That Toddlin' Town!

The first time I saw Chicago may have been after a short plane ride my family took up from Champaign in the early 1960s, when I was a boy. I'd have to ask my mom what year it was. And why we went. That I don't recall. Or where we stayed. And for how long. But I do recall that the plane, a little DC-3, I believe, had an actual hole in the cabin floor and you could see the ground and I asked my stepfather whether that was standard operating procedure and I was told nothing's perfect.

Certainly Chicago's not perfect. In 2012 it set a national record for murder, which ain't much to write home about. But I still think Chicago is the best American city. It has a feel that I didn't get in New York. Chicago is genuine, human, imposing, but not unavailable, if any of that makes sense. In New York I felt like everything had long been decided, but Chicago seems more fluid somehow. And I think Chicago is more attractive. Sure, New York has big and impressive buildings, but the ones in Chicago appeal to me more and in ways I find difficult to articulate. Chicago just feels *different* than New York and I much prefer that feeling. Pauline told me Chicago struck her as having a "continental cosmopolitan appeal" and she thought Chicagoans were quite friendly and real.

I've been to Chicago many times: among the visits were field trips in junior high school; when I was drafted for a physical; a wild adventure in the late 1970s with two buddies to see a Chicago Bulls/Boston Celtics game; a trip with a girlfriend to see Da Bears and the great Walter Payton; and in the summer of 2012 I took the train down from Kalamazoo to see my agent and we drank whiskey at the Billy Goat Tavern.

The Chicago story I chose to explore here is about the time I drove up from Champaign with my buddies Tom and Norm in Tom's bright-orange van. That damn van was so orange that I swear astronauts could see it from space. We had a case of Stroh's beer and drank half of it on the way up and so you can assume we were well lubed for the Windy City.

We eventually found our way to old Chicago Stadium where the Bulls played. During a timeout I went to the bathroom, and on the way back to grab beers for us, I discovered you could also buy mixed drinks in large plastic cups, and so I brought the boys whiskey, as if we really needed any more rocket fuel.

I think the Celtics won – it was one of those teams featuring big Dave Cowens at center, a player I always liked. After the game we ended up running bars downtown and taking on more rocket fuel – all in that damn orange van that could be seen from outer space. It's pretty miraculous that we somehow avoided accidents and cops. By the end of the night the three of us ended up sleeping on a floor at Tom's parents' in Berwyn and when we woke up the next morning, his father stood over us and said, "Looks like a bunch of drunken sailors."

You'd think we would have taken it easy after that, but we were pretty young and resilient, and despite the hangovers, a big breakfast got us recharged and that afternoon we went to a sort of Polish block party. Tom was Polish and Norm had some Polish blood, too. I recall we went into some house or a clubhouse the party had commandeered, and as we walked through the door, rather elderly Polish men handed us each shots of vodka.

More rocket fuel and off we went.

From there it was a blur and we drank with these old Polish guys who tried to teach me Polish words and it was all great fun. But what I remember best, though – and will never forget – was the moment when three elderly Polish women asked the three of us to dance with them. They led us to the dance floor and of course we didn't have any idea how to dance to whatever music it was and mostly we just flailed drunkenly, but our intentions were good.

A slower song came on and the woman I danced with attempted to teach me slow dancing and there was this crystal clear moment from the drunken haze when I glanced at her arm and saw numbers tattooed on it. I was pretty drunk and at first didn't really know what I was seeing.

Until I sat down again with Norm and Tom and it hit me: Those women – and many people in the room – were Polish Jews who had survived Hitler's concentration camps.

The next day, when we were sober again and driving the two hours back south to Champaign, I brought up the women and their tattooed arms and Tom and Norm said they, too, had noticed, but didn't know what to say at the time. We all glanced at each other and then for most of the trip home none of us said much at all.

Barreling Down the Homestretch

The Crazy Among Us
(Amerika, the Land of Nut Jobs, Wing
Nuts, and Wackos)

Back in the 1970s, I feared for America's future because of Nixon's shenanigans to essentially undermine democracy. Somehow we survived Nixon and for a long time I felt better about things. But then a disingenuous frat boy from Texas who resembles Alfred. E. Newman somehow got elected president with his lie about compassionate conservatives. And then all that angst Nixon had generated in me suddenly flared up. And it's going strong because once again the nation barely averted electing another rich boob who would have loved to undermine democracy before eventually going on to whatever planet is promised him by his beliefs and ensured by his magic underwear.

Too harsh?

Not harsh enough.

America is under siege by nut jobs, wing nuts, and whackos. Even though we avoided a dangerously divisive and inept Romney presidency, we're not home free by any means.

Sure, we just avoided the "fiscal cliff."

But for how long?

Folks, when the House of Representatives took its vote on the Senate deal to avoid the fiscal cliff, 167 members voted AGAINST basically saving the country.

Against!

Nut jobs, wing nuts, and whackos.

One-hundred and sixty-seven of them.

And they're everywhere.

Just look under a rock near you.

In Minnesota, it's Michelle Bachmann. She was actually re-elected – and how that is possible stumps me – but she was, and her first task was to once again introduce legislation to repeal what conservatives call Obamacare, even though the Supreme Court has confirmed it's the law of the land.

I hope all you Minnesotans feel you're getting your money's worth.

Down in Florida, shrill Allen West was defeated, but that likely won't stop him from using Fox "News" to continue his wild claims about communists in Congress or Obama as a Muslim socialist.

In South Carolina, Jim DeMint has resigned to cynically make millions heading a conservative think tank whose goal will be to try and make people think Obama is a tanned version of Hitler.

A conservative think tank?

Doesn't there first have to be the ability to think?

Folks, the House of Representatives is still controlled by people willing to shut down the government and damage America's credit rating to satisfy their desire to get rid of government altogether so states can teach that the earth is flat and everyone can basically just fend for themselves.

You know, like back in the days of cave people.

That comparison surely gives cave people a bad name.

And now, to update this chapter just a little, we have Donald Trump staring us in the face as the oddly resilient Republican frontrunner for president. Good God and General Jackson!

Though, I suppose Trump would say, "That's okay – just call me The Donald."

Random Thoughts on a Troubling Nation

Hugh Hefner:

I don't often think about Hugh Hefner (without needing a shower), even though, like me, he is an alum of the University of Illinois, and even though, in 1967, I was at the Illinois vs. Notre Dame football game in Champaign and we sat a few rows up from Hef and Barbie Benton. But isn't Hef about 127 by now? And isn't he a little old to still be climbing on top of twenty-one-year-old girls while on a Viagra IV? And isn't he finally old enough to wear something other than his pajamas?

Twenty-One-Year-Old Girls:

Are twenty-one-year-old girls smarter or dumber than when I was in my twenties? After all, some of them still let Hugh Hefner climb on top of them.

Michael Jackson:

The best proof so far that aliens have lived among us. But I suppose it's nice to know that some of them are good dancers.

Dennis Rodman:

The second-best proof that aliens live among us.

Newt Gingrich:

Never let that much gas and hot air near an open flame.

Lindsay Lohan:
Enough already!

Rush Limbaugh:
Proof that being a racist, misogynist, drug-addicted liar is actually a viable career choice.

Glenn Beck:
With Michael Jackson gone on to pedophilia hell, Glenn Beck is the best proof that aliens who vote Republican do indeed live among us.

Lance Armstrong:
Did it ever occur to him that just competing in Tour De France drug-free after surviving cancer would have been enough to earn enduring admiration?

Octomom:
At some point shouldn't an alarm go off and folks show up to tell Octomom that she has become too desperate to be famous for something, anything – even by California standards – and she just be placed under arrest or sentenced to live next door to Lance Armstrong?

The Media:
Someone in the media should be arrested and relocated next door to Lance Armstrong every time the media runs a story about Octomom or Lindsay Lohan.
Or the Kardashians.

Justin Bieber:
Again, why is this dude famous?

Michelle Bachmann:
No way I can put it any better than Jane Fonda's character on *The Newsroom* did: "Michelle Bachmann is a hair-do."

Oprah:
Isn't it illegal to practice TV psychiatry without a license?

Dr. Phil:
In the dictionary under 'blowhard' his photo should appear.

Ah-nold Schwarzenegger:
John Wayne on steroids.

John Wayne:
John Wayne on steroids.

Tom Cruise:
He's actually a pretty fair actor because he makes an audience believe his characters prefer women.

Katie Holmes:
Was it worth it?

Ashton Kutcher:
In the dictionary under "cad" his picture should appear.

The Macarena:
Instead of water-boarding, why not try this?

The 1950s:
Everyone's in a coma.

The 1960s:
The music mattered. And we woke up.

The 1970s:
Tin soldiers and Nixon's coming.

The 1980s:
The Lost Decade. The Myth of Reagan.

The 1990s:
Danger from the right. The coup of extremism.

The 2000s:
The jury's out. More knives sharpened on the right.

The NRA:
Hitler Youth, NRA. Hitler Youth, NRA. Hitler Youth, NRA. Keep repeating until you realize they're the same. Then use mouthwash and shower.

Wayne LaPierre:
He just needs to let a shock of hair fall more on his forehead, grow a little mustache, and chant, "Deutschland uber alles!" Mouthwash and shower. Twice.

Rick Santorum:
Has anyone ever been less tolerant while still claiming to be a Christian?

Mike Huckabee:
Yes – as a matter of fact, Huckabee somehow manages to be less tolerant than Santorum while claiming to be a Christian.

Bill O'Reilly:
Is "asshole" in the dictionary? If so, his picture goes there.

Fox News:
Joseph Goebbel's first choice to name his Nazi propaganda ministry, but he apparently passed, knowing the GOP would need the name.

Rick Perry:
Honestly, I never anticipated there'd be a Texas governor dumber than George W. Bush.

Texas:
Many Texans would like the state to secede. Let. Them. Go.

Oklahoma:
Conservatives there just passed a law against Sharia law. What are there, three Muslims in the whole state? What's next, a law against rational thought?

Mississippi:
Just passed a law against rational thought. Kidding! I think.

Arizona:
Isn't it just too damn hot to be asking people to show their papers?

Fifty Shades of Grey:
Really? You're kidding, right?

GOP Voter Suppression:

When GOP officials try to prevent people from voting they should be required to at least wear a swastika armband and goose-step.

The Kardashians:
Porky narcissistic chicks are hot? Go figure.

Donald Trump:
What would a love child from Trump and Sarah Palin be called? Godzilla with orange hair and a whiny, high-pitched voice?

Sarah Palin:
I know she's considered to be a hot MILF, but, sorry – willful ignorance is never sexy.

Reality TV:
The end of the world as we know it.

Whimsy and Translations

The latest reality TV show.
Translation: Annoying non-actors, with no talent, followed around with a camera doing nothing significant for gobs of money.

Atlanta mom shoots intruder in face five times.
Translation: He was apparently too ugly to merely smack with the broom.

Sushi tuna sells for $1.76 million.
Translation: People are really, really stupid.

Republican Sen. Mitch McConnell on "Meet the Press": "It's a shame that we have to use whatever leverage we have in Congress to get the president to deal with overspending."
Translation: We were happy to give the credit card to the boy king from Texas so he could destroy the economy, but, hey, that's a whites only credit card.

Porno plays during newscast.
Translation: The secret to high ratings.

California Boy Scout group seeks ban on gays.
Translation: Who do they think they are, the Catholic Church?

The Wisconsin Assembly routinely pushes debates and votes on contentious bills into the wee hours, when only lobbyists and the cleaning crew are left in the building.
Translation: It's none of the public's damn business what we Republicans do.

Texas lawmaker wants strippers to wear a license.
Translation: Because he apparently doesn't think that strippers realize they take their clothes off.

"We're all Arizonans now." –Sarah Palin, defending Arizona's new law cracking down on illegal immigration, May 15, 2010.
Translation: We're all stupid and narrow-minded bigots, just like Republican legislators in Arizona.

The Baseball Hall of Fame, which unveils its latest induction class Wednesday, has a membership that includes multiple virulent racists, drunks, and cheats
Translation: But, hey, in America, as long as you can hit a little ball you're A-Okay.

New Jersey Gov. Chris Christie (R) on *TODAY* said that despite New Jersey having some of the toughest gun laws in the country, that banning guns is not enough. "I'm willing to have that conversation," Christie said of a federal ban on powerful, high-capacity weapons, "but you've got to deal with these other issues."
Translation: Well, it's really sad those kids got killed, but I'm a Republican and we are owned by the NRA, and so while publicly I must express outrage over the killings and hope for it not to happen again, I'm not willing to actually resist my wacko, gun nut masters and do the right thing.

New Jersey cop spotted sleeping in car has gun stolen.
Translation: You know, one of those "good guys" the NRA wants stationed in every school.
Second Translation: Barney Fife Lives!

The Meaning of Life
(Thought I'd Set the Bar High)

So, here's the thing: life's a mystery. Unless of course you're Rick Santorum getting daily instructions by e-mail from God. Or Michelle Bachmann adjusting her tin foil crown to get better reception as God broadcasts daily to her bubble.

If only it were that easy.

A definite God.

Letting us know what's what and how it should be.

And available through e-mail and Facebook.

But that's not how it is.

We have to figure things out on our own.

And there's much we just can't seem to figure out.

Faith, I know, is supposed to help. I don't discount that. Faith in something is a good thing. We all need something to believe in. Faith matters. Faith can be reassuring. It can guide us. Life's hard enough without concluding that nothing matters.

You'd become no better than The Misfit in Flannery O'Connor's story *A Good Man is Hard to Find* without some sense of faith. The Misfit concludes that there is no God or heaven and so no consequences. And if there are no consequences, then murder and all sorts of mayhem can be viewed as not much different than buying soda in a store.

And to be sure, we have plenty of folks who believe capitalism is a faith and sadly some practice it like The Misfit – without an understanding or concern for consequences. Greed achieved at any cost becomes their faith.

And a tsunami cresting against the rest of us.

It's hard to know what to believe in. I'm willing to entertain the possibility that there is something greater than humans that somehow is integrally involved in the fate of humans.

A God?

I don't know. And neither do Bachmann and Santorum, despite their arrogant claims. They are snake-oil salespeople hiding being a perverted notion of faith in order to achieve intolerant political ends.

I know this (or rather I suspect it since there's much I can't know): A benevolent God – a God like many faiths describe – would not tolerate the intolerance of a Bachmann or a Santorum and the hypocritical religious charlatans that prostitute faith for personal gain.

For all of Bachmann's and Santorum's claims of religious superiority, their intolerance makes me think they are actually Godless.

And a God that would favor the intolerance of a Bachmann or a Santorum would not be a God worth following.

So, who and what is God, if indeed there is a God?

Is God male? I try not to assume, but I think Bachmann and Santorum believe God is male because they appear to believe men rightly occupy a higher status in life than women. Sort of like managers and workers. Masters and slaves.

Weren't women created from men, the Bible claims, thus making them, what – mascots?

Property?

Certainly the war on women being perpetuated by the Republican Party is evidence that they don't believe women to be the equal of men.

But I promise not to digress too far into politics and instead try to stay in the realm of a philosophical examination of this very odd existence we call life.

The whole notion of an all-knowing, all-everything God seems to make the notion of gender irrelevant. Sorry Rick and Michelle. But if something that far beyond our ability to grasp and understand, an architect of all we see and also all we are yet to see, would not be limited by gender, would it?

Notice I use *it* rather than he or she.

Now, all this raises some troubling questions. Why does God need to be so anonymous, so out of sight, so behind the scenes? And why do TV evangelists insist that God wants them, the folks selling the snake oil, to be rich before God can work the magic?

Why is God involved in acquiring material possessions at all?

Captain Kirk put it pretty well in *Star Trek V* when he asked, "What does God need with a starship?"

More troubling questions:

Why did God permit the Holocaust?

Or Pearl Harbor?

Or 911?

Or disco?

I won't accept that we have to blindly acknowledge that God has a plan. It's more fluid than that. Rigid obedience subtracts the human element from the equation. It ought to be a partnership.

Otherwise, we're slaves.

What if God is not actually nice and benevolent?

Instead, malevolent.

What if the Mormons are wrong and God isn't out there in space manipulating the known universe and creating estates for them?

Or is that what Scientologists believe?

I confess that sometimes I get my religious fantasies mixed up.

What if God, the creator of all we know to be real, and all we hope will be real, is actually no better than Tony Soprano?

Or is as nuts and narcissistic as Donald Trump?

After all, God permitted the Holocaust, Pearl Harbor, 911.

And disco.

The Persistence of Memory
(Thanks for the Title, Mr. Dali)

I should have known better than to set myself up to follow God, but here goes. This book started on the note of memory as a bit of a mystery, like God.

And so it's fitting to conclude with memory.

My memories come and go. Some are foggy. Some quite clear. Which ones should we trust most – foggy or clear?

Sometimes a sound or smell can spark a memory.

I have a special memory. Special not because it's about a special or noteworthy event.

But special, I suppose, because for much of my life it has come to me at various times.

Almost always this memory is sparked when it's quiet and in my head I hear a noise that resembles a soft hiss.

Not like a cat.

Not like air escaping a tire.

Something quieter than those.

Something softer.

And it allows me to instantly step into the special memory.

Hiss.

And off I go.

The memory's scene: my grandmother's kitchen in Jonesboro, Arkansas.

After I was born, it would have been one of the first places I saw once I was taken home from the hospital, though my memories do not go back that far.

Next to a doorway from the kitchen to the next room, which was a bedroom, there was a small gas heater standing perhaps two feet high.

It emitted a low, soft, quiet hiss.

Hiss.

I can still see the blue-orange flames, tiny flames.

Why do I remember this?

I don't know.

And likely that matters not at all.

But when something sparks me to step back into this memory, I can see the kitchen in remarkable, vivid detail.

The house is no longer there. Torn down in a year many years ago. My grandparents then moved to the house next door, which I can also visualize fairly well, though not as well as the kitchen in their old house.

The original house had been, frankly, primitive. There was no indoor toilet and we used an outhouse, which was startling to my sister and I because we were then growing up in a suburban house in a northern college town. My mother and stepfather eventually built my grandparents an indoor bathroom with a shower and bathtub. It was the nicest room in the whole house.

But visiting that house as a kid was fun because everything about the house and people and the town were so different – so *Southern*. Exotic in a vaguely primitive way. I do recall that my grandparents voted for George Wallace for president and then Jimmy Carter. I believe the Confederate battle flag was on their car's chrome bumper.

I feel sure it was on someone's bumper, if not theirs.

My mother grew up in that house during World War II. She told me that at one time one of the rickety shacks across the street – Culberhouse Street – had been a whorehouse. During the war, I believe. The house next to my grandparent's house was where my mother was when she heard the news about Pearl Harbor. She was sitting on the porch with other kids listening to the radio when the news was announced. During the war she sometimes walked past a prisoner of war camp in Jonesboro that housed German prisoners. It was full of blond-headed boys who in some cases were not so much older than she was. My mother's maiden name was very German and she sometimes got teased about it during the war.

But back to the memory.

Hiss.

If you entered the kitchen from the bedroom doorway and not through the back door, the first thing you saw was the back door and shelves with curtains next to the door. My grandfather kept personal items on the shelves, such as a kit he used to shine his shoes. I think he kept his whiskey bottle in there, too. The refrigerator was just before you reached the shelves. To the left of the back door was the sink, and to the left of that were counters interrupted by a window with a view of the rear of a gas station building until you had swiveled completely back to the way you came in and the stove was on the right, next to the little hissing heater. On the counter between the heater and stove – a bread box. The table and chairs were in the center of the room.

Why do I recall the kitchen when I hear a sound like the one the heater made?

A mystery.

I may never know.

Do I need to know?

I think not.

But I speculate this: I first heard that gentle hiss that was not as angry as a hissing cat, nor as insistent as air escaping a tire, when I was very young indeed.

A baby.

Too young to have had worries.

When I was alive but did not think about being alive.

When I was alive without effort.

A time with no complications.

Before I learned to fear and to worry and to know that some people can't be trusted and some can and you must learn the difference as soon as you can.

That might be why I have that memory from time to time.

And have had it all my life.

It's a refuge memory.

I can step back into that memory and for a time, too brief of a time, I can remember when being alive didn't require effort, or worry, or fear.

It's a memory of the time of the beginning, before we started fretting about endings.

Hiss.

But a good hiss.

Epilogue

I didn't plan to write an epilogue, but most of this book was written nearly three years ago, and three years is an eternity in the American cyclorama of preventable violence, willful ignorance (See Sarah Palin), mindless celebrity worship (See the Kardashian Cult), and entrenched greed (See GOP). There's been another school shooting, just days ago at the time of this writing, at an Oregon college, and with the predictable aftermath:

A sea of lit candles.

Much hand wringing and anguish.

A river of tears.

Parents and classmates moan for the dead.

A Republican presidential candidate – Jeb! – dismisses the event as, "Stuff happens."

Another Republican 'presidential candidate' – The Donald! – echoes Jeb!

A domestic terrorist organization – The NRA! – prepares its press releases calling for even more guns and "good guys with guns!" in classrooms.

President Obama flashes real anger and reminds us that, sadly, we are used to these bloodlettings, which somehow, some way, must be stopped, but can't because the NRA owns enough of Congress to prevent sensible gun regulations. It owns enough of Congress to even prevent sensible thought and debate. It owns enough of Congress to suppress facts and reality. It keeps the door open for another Oregon, and another, and another, and another...

There will be no sensible gun regulations. None. Nada. Instead, The Republican Congress and presidential candidates will quickly hijack the national attention span, which is less than that of a gnat, and distract us away from Oregon – and the coming next mass shooting, already hatching in some deranged mind – with more fake "scandals," such as Benghazi and Planned Parenthood.

The public will quickly – likely already has – shift its attention back to the latest frothy blather from The Kardashians. Or back to Caitlyn Jenner, a brave person indeed, but one who, in embracing true identity, remains otherwise mostly in pursuit of easy TV money in exchange for salacious gossip, and who remains aligned with a Republican Party that does not want the likes of her.

Many Americans – millions, sadly – won't have to sadly turn away from school shootings at all because they are disciples of the fraudulent fakery of Fox News, and so – like Jeb! – they know that stuff happens! And that it has nothing to do with them at all. Shed tears over an Oregon school shooting? That's for lightweights and squishy liberals! The Fox Folks are consumed with the certainty that somehow Hillary Clinton personally shot our ambassador in Benghazi and then covered it up while also selling baby parts (in dark alleys, no doubt) supplied to her by Planned Parenthood.

The coming presidential race between Hillary's emails and whichever clown the GOP coronates to keep cutting taxes on rich folks will be a raucous, bruising, expensive Armageddon; and all that's at stake is whether America goes forward and keeps democracy and at least a notion of fairness and equality among classes, or slips back to the 1920s and finally becomes a corporate theocracy of sorts launching perpetual wars.

But, other than that – everything is hunky-dory!

Stuff happens!

I leave you with the sage advice of Elwood P. Dowd, a mere character in a play, often accompanied by an invisible, six-foot rabbit named Harvey, but Elwood is a character wiser than many real people and all the Republicans running for emperor/president:

"Years ago my mother used to say to me, she'd say, 'In this world, Elwood, you must be' – she always called me Elwood – 'In this world, Elwood, you must be oh so smart or oh so pleasant.' Well, for years I was smart. I recommend pleasant. You may quote me."